BUILD IT!

Caroline Alliston

Quarto is the authority on a wide range of topics.

Quarto educates, entertains and enriches the lives of our readers—enthusiasts and lovers of hands-on living.

www.quartoknows.com

Developed and written by: Caroline Alliston
MA(Cantab), MSc, CEng FIMechE
Illustrator: Tom Connell
Photograper: Michael Wicks
Model maker: Fiona Hayes
Consultants: John Harvey BEng, CEng MIMechE,
Dr Alex Alliston MA(Cantab), CEng MIMechE
Design and editorial: Starry Dog Books Ltd
QED Project Editor: Carly Madden
QED Designer: Mike Henson

First published in the UK in 2017 by
QED Publishing
Part of The Quarto Group
The Old Brewery
6 Blundell Street
London, N7 9BH

Website information is correct at time of going to press. However, the publishers cannot accept liability for any information or links found on any Internet sites, including third-party websites.

A catalogue record for this book is available from the British Library.

ISBN 978-1-78493-848-2

Printed in China

MIX
Paper from
responsible sources
FSC® C016973
www.fsc.org

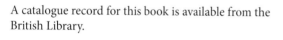

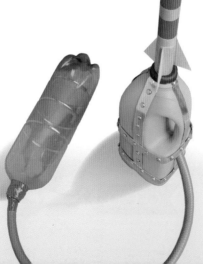

FOREWORD

- -

Be inspired to make our world a better place.

We live in a 'made' world. Without the advances made by engineers and scientists, we simply would not have houses, cars, food and drink, clothes, healthcare and entertainment. Today we face truly global challenges, such as feeding a growing population and coping with climate change.

This book provides 25 exciting and engaging projects to encourage creative thinking and problem solving. I hope it will inspire the next generation of engineers and scientists that is needed to make our world a better place.

Dr Colin Brown CEng FIMechE, FIMMM,
Director of Engineering, Institution of
Mechanical Engineers

CONTENTS

HANDY AT HOME

MAKING LIGHT WORK!

PROGRAM ME!

BE INSPIRED!

Test your design, creativity and engineering skills with these 25 exciting projects and challenges.

WORK SAFELY

Always get permission from an adult before beginning a project and ask for their help when necessary.

SCISSORS
Be careful not to cut yourself with scissors. If using nail scissors, don't spike yourself – ask an adult to start the cut for you.

WOODEN SKEWERS
To avoid injuries, cut about 5 mm off the sharp tips, leaving the sticks slightly pointed to help you assemble the models.

GLUE GUNS
Only use low melt temperature glue guns; high melt glue guns can burn you badly. Use a gluing mat to protect your table. Avoid getting glue on your clothes. Make sure your hands and gluing area are dry before you switch on your glue gun. If you don't have a glue gun, most of the models can be made using double-sided foam sticky tape – see 'From Your Toolbox' on page 10 for details.

MAINS ELECTRICITY
Always check that the socket is switched off before you plug in or unplug an electrical appliance. Check that the mains cable of your glue gun is not damaged before you plug it in.

JUNIOR HACKSAWS AND DRILLS
Make sure you clamp your work in the vice so that you don't cut your fingers.

BRADAWLS AND SHARP PENCILS
Be careful not to spike yourself with bradawls and sharp pencils, and don't put them near your eyes.

SPINNING PROPELLERS
Be careful not to put these near your eyes or hair. Don't put fingers in the way of the blades.

CABLE TIES
Be careful not to fasten cable ties around your fingers.

GET READY

Before you start a project, make sure you have to hand all the tools and materials that you'll need – each project has its own YOU WILL NEED list. Then read the easy-to-follow, illustrated step-by-step instructions to find out how to make the models. Discover more in the NOW YOU CAN activities and HOW IT WORKS explanations.

Cheap, everyday and recycled household objects are used wherever possible. Collect old CDs and DVDs, polystyrene foam pizza discs, corks, plastic milk bottle lids and plastic drinks bottles.

Wood and fasteners can be bought from builders' merchants. Electrical projects reuse the same parts where possible, so once you have finished with one model, you can take it apart and make another!

TAKE CARE!

Look out for the 'Take Care!' symbol, which refers you to the warning instructions on the first page of each project. Craft knives, power tools and secateurs should only be used by an adult.

DIFFICULTY LEVELS

The projects fall into three categories ranging from easier to more advanced:

DIFFICULTY LEVEL ▶▶▶▶ 1

Eight fun projects to get your engineering skills in gear.

DIFFICULTY LEVEL ▶▶▶▶ 2

Eleven exciting projects and challenges to test your creativity.

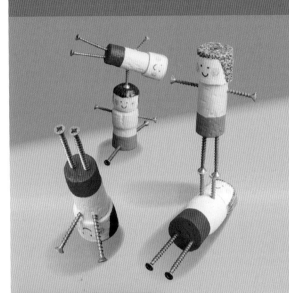

DIFFICULTY LEVEL ▶▶▶▶ 3

Six amazing projects for the more experienced budding engineer.

WHERE TO BUY PARTS

Electrical parts are described on pages 8 and 98. Here are some useful suppliers of bought-in parts:

- spiratronics.com/technology for fun cn.html
- redfernelectronics.co.uk
- rapidonline.com
- tts-group.co.uk
- technobotsonline.com
- mindsetsonline.co.uk

MOTOR AND BULB CIRCUITS

YOU WILL NEED:

These are the electrical parts (components) you will need to make the motor and bulb circuits.

1 PP3 battery clip

1 battery holder 2 x AA

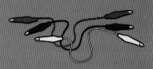

3 crocodile leads

1 toggle switch (SPST)

**2 AA cells
(zinc chloride or similar)**

**1 3V motor,
about 5,000 rpm
(revolutions per minute)**

**1 MES bulb holder with
3V bulb screwed in**

Here's how to make the circuits for the vibrating brush monster, fan boat, handheld fan, torch and steady hand game.

1 Take a crocodile lead. Clip one end onto the metal end of the red wire from the battery clip. Clip the other end to one of the terminals on the toggle switch.

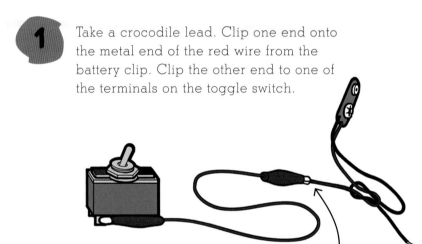

Metal end

2 Take a second crocodile lead and clip one end onto one of the motor (or bulb holder) terminals and the other end onto the unused switch terminal.

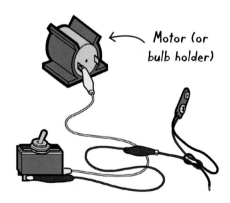

Motor (or bulb holder)

3 Clip one end of the third crocodile lead to the black wire from the battery clip. Clip the other end to the unused bulb holder (or motor) terminal.

Clip to metal end.

Connect here for steady hand game.

Connect here for torch.

4 Attach the battery clip firmly to the battery holder. Fit the cells into the battery holder, making sure the flat end of each cell is pushed against a spring.

Bulb holder (or motor)

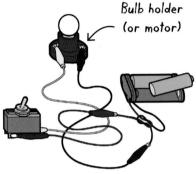

5 Switch on and check the motor shaft is rotating (or bulb is lit). Switch off and check the motor stops (or bulb goes off).

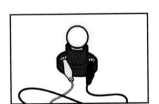

6 If the circuit doesn't work, try pressing the wires from the battery directly onto the motor/bulb holder terminals. If this works, start reintroducing the other parts.

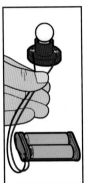

HOW TO AVOID SHORT CIRCUITS

- Never connect the wires from the battery clip directly together – they must be connected via the motor or bulb.

- Do not use alkaline or rechargeable cells – these get very hot when short circuited.

- Tie the wires from the battery clip in a reef knot so the metal ends point away from each other.

Reef knot

Metal ends

- Make sure the plastic sleeves (insulators) cover the crocodile clips to prevent the metal parts (conductors) touching accidentally.

Crocodile clip

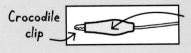

Plastic sleeve

CD RACER

Wind up the rubber band and set your CD racer speeding across the floor.

YOU WILL NEED:

1 cotton reel

2 old CDs/DVDs

rubber bands (different sizes)
1 mm thick x 3–4 mm wide
x 7–9 cm long

1 rubber

1 M10 washer
plastic (preferably)
or metal

1 pencil

FROM YOUR TOOLBOX:

• sandpaper • low melt glue gun or double-sided foam sticky tape (12 mm wide x 1 mm thick, super-sticky recommended) • skewer or wire paper clip

Remove any paper labels from the ends of the cotton reel. Stick a CD onto one end.

 Stick the second CD onto the other end of the cotton reel.

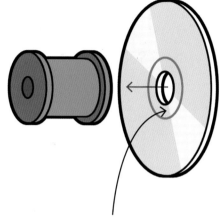

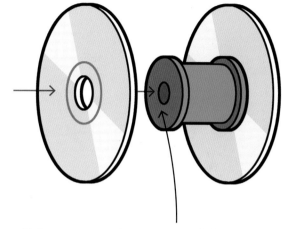

Roughening the surface of the CD slightly with sandpaper will help the glue to stick.

Make sure the holes in the middle line up and are not blocked with glue or tape.

 Thread a rubber band through the central hole, leaving loops sticking out on either side.

 Push the rubber through one of the loops in the rubber band.

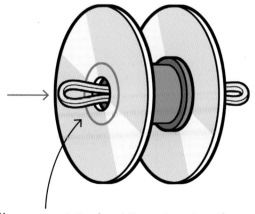

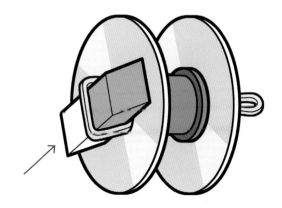

You can push the band through with a skewer or pull it with a hook made from a paper clip.

5 Push the other end of the rubber band through the washer, leaving a loop sticking out.

6 Push the pencil through the loop in the rubber band that's next to the washer.

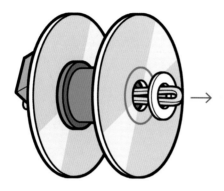

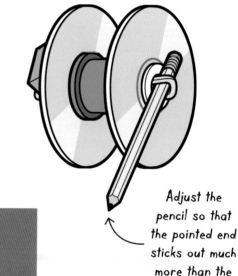

Adjust the pencil so that the pointed end sticks out much more than the other end.

TIPS & HINTS...

The rubber band should be just loose before you start winding it up with the pencil. If your rubber band is tight, swap it for a longer one, otherwise the extra friction will slow your racer down. If it is too loose, try a shorter band.

7 To wind up your CD racer, hold the rubber with one hand and use the other hand to turn the pencil round about ten to fifteen times. Feel the resistance increasing as you turn the pencil.

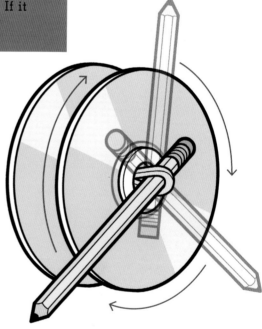

8 Place your CD racer on a smooth surface with the pencil pointing backwards. Let go and watch the racer go speeding across the floor!

If you don't turn the pencil enough times, the CD racer won't go far. If you turn it too many times, the rubber band may snap.

HOW IT WORKS

The CD racer converts elastic potential energy in the wound-up rubber band into movement (kinetic) energy as the rubber band unwinds, making the racer move across the floor. Energy is also converted into heat and sound due to friction between the moving parts.

As the rubber band unwinds, it turns the rubber (made from a high friction material that grips well), and as the rubber turns, the CD unit turns with it. The washer has low friction, allowing the CD unit to turn while the pencil stays pointing the same way. The tip of the pencil has quite low friction, allowing it to slide easily across a smooth surface.

NOW YOU CAN...

* Wind up the rubber band by different amounts and compare how far the racer travels.

* Experiment with different lengths or widths of rubber band to try and improve your racer's performance.

* Sharpen the pencil or adjust it so that it sticks out more or less.

* Change the washer material or lubricate it with washing-up liquid or bicycle oil to reduce friction.

* Test the CD racer on different surfaces.

* Challenge a friend to a Formula One CD race!

ROCKING AND ROLLING

BALANCING GYMNASTS

Make your acrobatic gymnasts perform fantastic balancing acts.

YOU WILL NEED:

8 corks, preferably plastic

7 countersunk Pozidriv® screws
4-mm thread x 40 mm long
(size 8 x 1½")

10 countersunk Pozidriv® screws
4-mm thread x 50 mm long
(size 8 x 2")

8 countersunk Pozidriv® screws
4-mm thread x 30 mm long
(size 8 x 1¼")

FROM YOUR TOOLBOX:

• vice • junior hacksaw
• bradawl or sharp pencil
• drill and 4-mm-diameter drill bit • Pozidriv® screwdriver • permanent marker pen

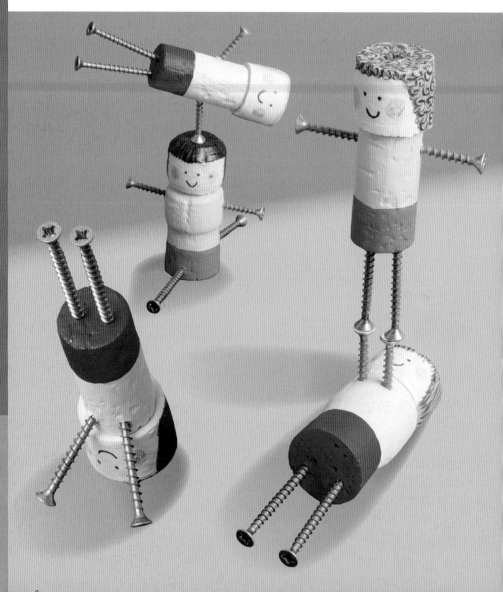

⚠ **TAKE CARE** using the saw and drill – ask an adult for help.

1 ⚠️ Saw a cork in half. Indent the tops, then drill a hole through each half. Attach each half cork to a whole cork by screwing a 40-mm screw through the holes.

Draw a face on each of your gymnasts.

2 To make the 'top' gymnast, screw the 50-mm screws straight up into the body, then screw the 30-mm screws into the sides.

Adjust the screws until it stands up without falling over.

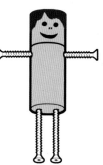

3 To make the 'base' gymnast, screw in the arms (use two 30-mm screws) and legs (use 50-mm screws), as shown.

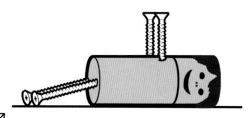

Make sure the 'feet' touch the ground and the arms stick up straight and are the same length.

4 Balance the top gymnast on the base gymnast. If it falls off, adjust the screws until the top gymnast balances.

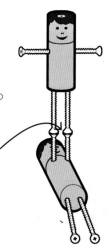

The weight of the 'top' needs to be directly above here to balance.

NOW YOU CAN...

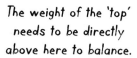

* Make a gymnast do a headstand. Use 40-mm screws for the arms.

HOW IT WORKS

The lower gymnast has to provide a stable, level base for the other gymnast to balance on. The centre of gravity of the top gymnast needs to be directly above this base.

* Make one gymnast doing the splits and another in the 'flag' position, and balance them as shown. You may need to adjust the top gymnast's arm to get it to balance.

BALLOON BUGGY

YOU WILL NEED:

1 sheet of corrugated cardboard or plastic (2–3 mm thick)

2 straight plastic drinking straws

1 length of garden hose or plastic tube, about 1.5-cm diameter x 24 cm long

Cable ties/zip ties 10–20 cm long

2 wooden skewers

4 plastic milk bottle lids

1 round party balloon

Lightweight decorations e.g. feathers, tinsel (optional)

FROM YOUR TOOLBOX:

• sharp pencil • ruler • large scissors • low melt glue gun or double-sided foam sticky tape • pencil sharpener • poster tack • secateurs

Make a balloon buggy that whizzes along the ground.

16

1 Draw a rectangle on your corrugated sheet as shown and cut it out. This will be the base of the buggy.

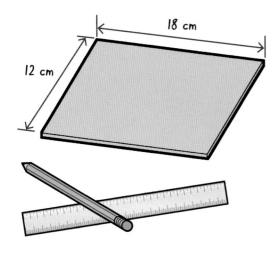

2 Draw a line across each end of the card, 2 cm in from the edges. Stick two 14-cm-long straws onto the lines.

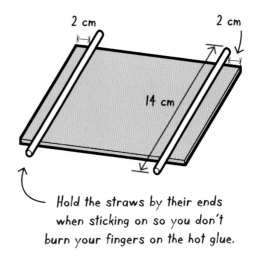

Hold the straws by their ends when sticking on so you don't burn your fingers on the hot glue.

3 Turn the base over and attach the hose. The curved ends must point upwards to prevent the balloon rubbing on the ground.

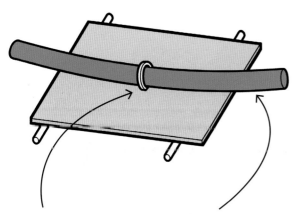

Pierce two holes in the base. Fasten the hose on firmly with a cable tie.

If the hose has curved ends, make sure they point upwards.

4 Use the scissors to cut off the sharp tips of the wooden skewers. Sharpen the blunt ends slightly – this will help the wheels to go on.

Just cut off the very tip so you don't spike yourself.

5 Push each plastic milk bottle lid, open end downwards, onto a lump of poster tack. Use a sharp pencil to make a hole in the middle of each one.

 6 Slide the skewers (axles) through the straws. Push the lids on to the skewers until they almost touch the ends of the straws. Ask an adult to cut off the skewer ends with secateurs.

Don't make the hole too big - it will need to be a tight fit on the skewer.

Keep the pencil upright or the lead may snap.

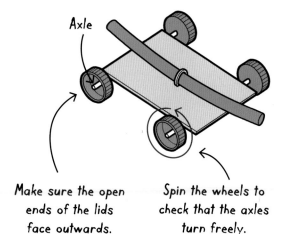

Axle

Make sure the open ends of the lids face outwards.

Spin the wheels to check that the axles turn freely.

7 Slide the balloon onto the hose. Blow through the other end to inflate the balloon, squeeze the neck, place on a smooth floor, then let go.

8 You can colour or paint your buggy, or add some lightweight decorations, such as feathers.

If the balloon comes off while blowing up, attach the neck to the tube with a cable tie.

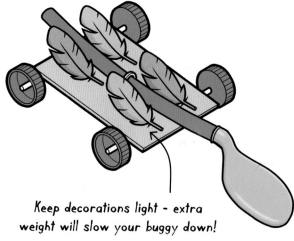

Keep decorations light - extra weight will slow your buggy down!

NOW YOU CAN...

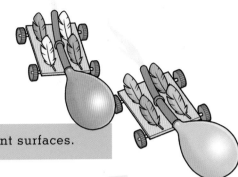

* ✱ Challenge a friend to see whose buggy travels the furthest.

* ✱ Test your buggy on different surfaces.

* ✱ Try using different tube diameters or different sizes and shapes of balloon to see which work best.

* ✱ Make changes to the buggy to stop the balloon rubbing on the ground.

* ✱ Repair your buggy! If the straws come loose, secure them with cable ties – but don't pull the ties too tight or you'll stop the axles rotating freely.

HOW IT WORKS

- -

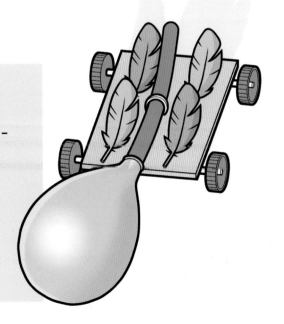

Compressed air is stored in the balloon. When you release the neck of the balloon, a jet of air is pushed out of the other end of the tube. This acts like a rocket, pushing the buggy forwards. The surface the buggy is on needs to be smooth. If there's too much friction, the air jet won't be able to overcome it and the buggy won't move.

ROCKING AND ROLLING

MARBLE MAZE

Design a tricky marble maze, full of false trails and dead ends.

YOU WILL NEED:

1 board e.g. MDF, hardboard or plywood
roughly 3 mm thick
x 30 cm x 30 cm

4 m square section wood
1 cm or 1.2 cm square

1 marble

FROM YOUR TOOLBOX:

• sandpaper • ruler • pencil
• vice • junior hacksaw
• low melt glue gun • sheet
of A3 paper

⚠ TAKE CARE using the saw – ask an adult for help.

AIM OF THE GAME...

The aim is to tilt the board and make the marble roll its way through the maze without getting stuck in the false trails.

1 Measure and cut four edge pieces. Smooth with sandpaper and glue them to the base.

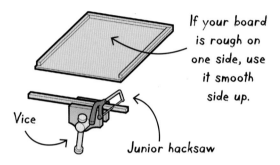

If your board is rough on one side, use it smooth side up.

Vice

Junior hacksaw

2 On paper, design a maze in which the marble has to travel around most of the board.

Include false trails with dead ends or gaps slightly too small for the marble.

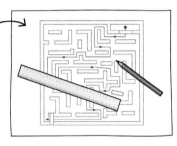

3 Prepare each piece of wood in turn and glue it on, checking the gap size with the marble.

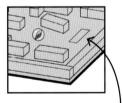

Mark the position before gluing so the piece ends up in the right place.

4 Try out the maze – check the marble runs along the real trail but not the false trails.

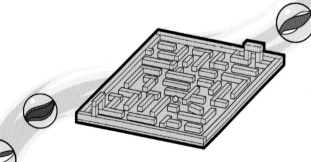

HOW IT WORKS

When you tilt the board, the marble rolls downhill due to gravity – a force that pulls things towards the ground. Adjust the direction of tilt to make the marble roll around the obstacles.

NOW YOU CAN...

✱ Mark the start and finish with arches or labels.

✱ Challenge friends to see who can finish fastest.

0:00

21

YOU WILL NEED:

1 board e.g. corrugated cardboard, MDF or hardboard 3–4 mm thick x 40 cm x 60 cm

2 strips corrugated cardboard 6 cm x 60 cm

2 strips corrugated cardboard 6 cm x 40 cm

1 marble

1 or 2 plastic drinks bottles

Variety of materials such as cardboard tubes, corrugated cardboard or plastic, packaging material etc

FROM YOUR TOOLBOX:

• low melt glue gun • large scissors • nail scissors • sticky tape • sandpaper • stopwatch

22

ROCKING AND ROLLING
MARBLE RUN

- -

Can your marble zigzag down the track and meet the 10-second challenge?

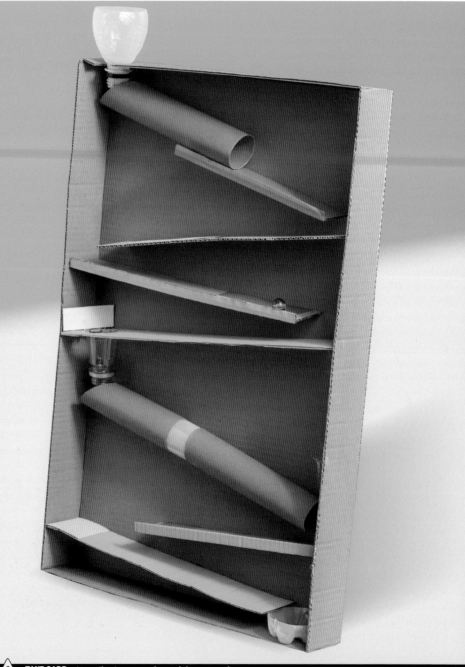

⚠ **TAKE CARE** using nail scissors – ask an adult to start the cut.

THE CHALLENGE...

1. The marble must travel from the top to the bottom of the run in as close to 10 seconds as possible.
2. Your run must be no more than 60 cm high and 40 cm wide.
3. You can take as long as you like to build your marble run.

1 Glue the four strips of corrugated cardboard to the edges of the board, as shown. These will stop the marble falling off the sides.

2 Design and make a stand for your marble run and glue it to the back of the board.

Can you think of a way to make the stand adjustable so that you can alter the tilt and change the speed of the marble?

Glue the edges together.

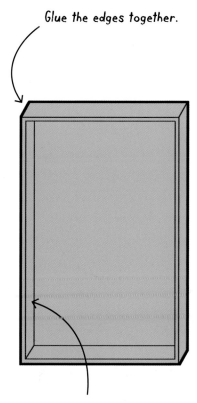

The edges will help to stiffen the board if it is made of cardboard.

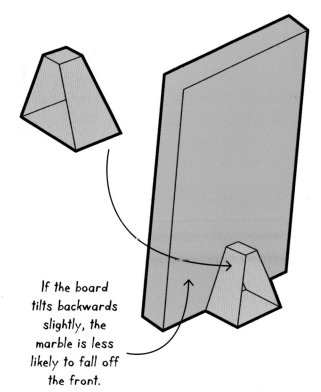

If the board tilts backwards slightly, the marble is less likely to fall off the front.

3

 Using nail scissors, cut the top off a plastic bottle to make a funnel. Cut away an arch shape from the top cardboard strip and glue the funnel in place.

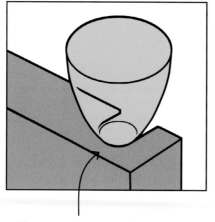

The arch shape should just fit the neck of the bottle.

4 Make a track down the board for the marble. Try out each section before adding the next. Include lots of strips at shallow angles.

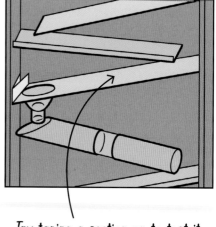

Try taping a section on to test it before gluing it in place.

 5 Stick rough surfaces to the strips to slow the marble down. If your marble falls off, add front edges to the strips.

Sandpaper   *Front edge*   *Cut the bottom off a plastic bottle to make a marble catcher.*

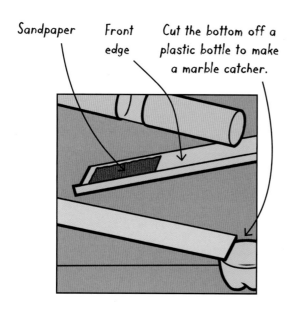

6 Now time how long it takes for the marble to travel from the top to the bottom of your marble run.

How close can you get to 10 seconds?

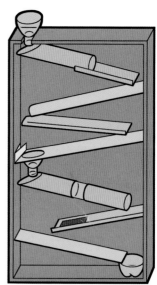

HOW IT WORKS

The marble is pulled downwards by gravity. If allowed to fall freely, it would take only a fraction of a second to fall the height of the board. You have slowed it down by making it travel further, stop and change direction, and by using different slopes. Using rough or bumpy materials also slows it down.

NOW YOU CAN...

Make some changes to get even closer to the target time of 10 seconds.

* Alter the slope of some of the strips to slow down or speed up the marble.

* Modify the stand to alter the tilt of the marble run.

* Change the surfaces of some strips. If you've used corrugated cardboard strips, try removing some of the top surface so that the marble runs on the bumpy corrugations.

* Put in small ramps and jumps.

* Try adding a 'loop the loop'!

ROCKING AND ROLLING

VIBRATING BRUSH MONSTER

Amaze your friends by turning a dustpan brush into a scuttling monster!

YOU WILL NEED:

For the circuit:
• 1 battery clip • 1 battery holder • 3 crocodile leads • 1 toggle switch • 1 motor • 2 AA cells

1 wood offcut
1–1.2 cm thick x 3–3.5 cm wide x 7 cm long

1 motor mount
(plastic, self-adhesive)

1 wide dustpan brush with stiff, sloping bristles

6 cable ties / zip ties
20–30 cm long

Googly eyes

Decorations
e.g. pipe cleaners, feathers

FROM YOUR TOOLBOX:

• pencil • ruler • junior hacksaw • vice • sandpaper • plastic bottle lid (3-cm diameter) • wood file • drill with 2-mm-diameter drill bit • scissors • double-sided foam tape • low melt glue gun (optional for decorations)

⚠ **TAKE CARE** using the saw and drill – ask an adult for help.

1 Using the battery clip, battery holder, crocodile leads, toggle switch, motor and AA cells, follow the steps on pages 8–9 to connect up your motor circuit.

2 ⚠ To make the motor spacer, mark and saw off a 2.5-cm length of wood. Smooth the rough edges with sandpaper.

3 ⚠ Draw round the bottle lid on the remaining wood. Saw around the circle roughly, then round it off using the file.

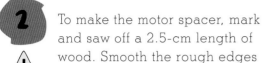

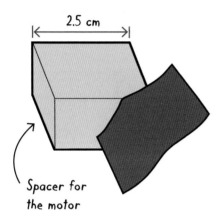

Spacer for
the motor

Mark the
centre of
the disc.

4 ⚠ Mark four holes on the disc, as shown, then clamp the disc in the vice and drill right through. Hold the drill straight or you may get an oversized hole or snap the drill bit.

5 Pick a hole and push the motor shaft into it – it needs to be a tight fit or the disc will fly off.

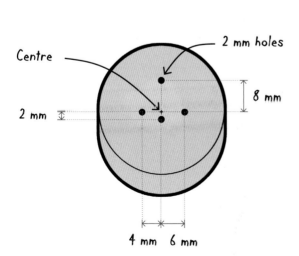

Centre

2 mm holes

2 mm

8 mm

4 mm   6 mm

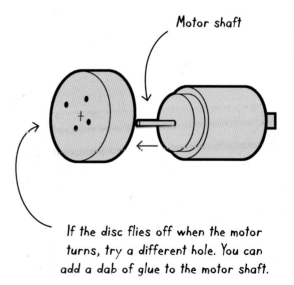

Motor shaft

If the disc flies off when the motor
turns, try a different hole. You can
add a dab of glue to the motor shaft.

Clip the motor into the motor mount, as shown.

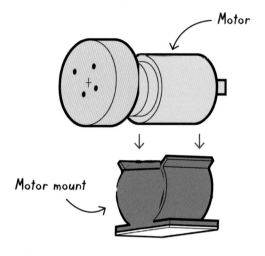

Motor

Motor mount

 Stick the mount firmly to the spacer. Then stick two strips of double-sided foam tape to the bottom of the spacer.

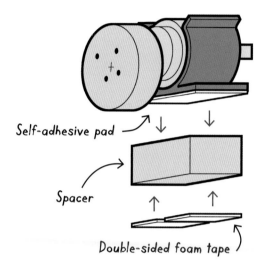

Self-adhesive pad

Spacer

Double-sided foam tape

 Stick the spacer to the top of the brush, as shown. The brush needs to be quite wide so that it won't fall over.

Motor assembly

1.5 cm

Stick the motor assembly about 1.5 cm in from the end of the brush. If it's any closer to the end, the cable tie that you attach in step 10 may slide off.

 To check that the disc won't hit the spacer, the motor mount or the top of the brush, turn it all the way round.

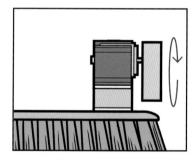

TIPS & HINTS...

If the disc hits the spacer or motor mount, slide the motor forward in its mount. If it hits the top of the brush, use a smaller offset distance or disc diameter or a thicker spacer.

10 Feed a cable tie through the bristles without bending them. Use it to attach the motor assembly firmly to the brush.

 11 Stick the battery next to the spacer using double-sided foam tape. Cable-tie the battery unit and crocodile leads in place.

Crocodile leads go under the cable tie so they don't vibrate off the motor contacts.

If your cable tie is too short, join two together.

12 If your brush handle has a hole, remove the nut and on/off label from the switch and push the cylindrical part up through the hole. Put the label back and screw the nut down firmly.

13 If the handle doesn't have a hole, mount the switch on its side next to the battery using foam tape and cable ties, as shown.

Cable-tie the switch and leads.

Make sure the switch is firmly attached.

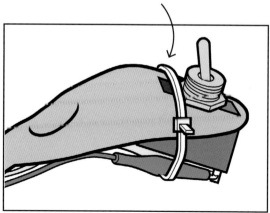

Try out your vibrating brush on a smooth floor to make sure that it works.

 Fold the wires neatly under the handle and cable tie them in place. Snip off the ends of the ties – but don't snip the wires!

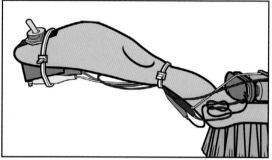

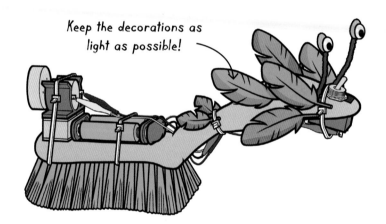

16 Now turn your brush into a monster! Add some lightweight decorations such as pipe cleaners and feathers, then attach some googly eyes.

Keep the decorations as light as possible!

HOW IT WORKS

Slide the bristles of your brush over your hand first one way and then the other. If the bristles are sloping, you should feel that they move more easily one way than the other. Because the wooden disc is mounted using an off-centre hole, the centre of gravity keeps moving up and down (and from side to side) as the disc turns, making the brush vibrate. When the brush tries to move one way due to the vibrations, the bristles tend to dig in and prevent it. When it tries to move the other way, the bristles slide easily across a smooth surface, so the brush moves in this direction.

NOW YOU CAN...

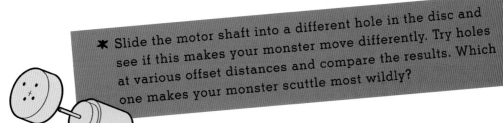

★ Slide the motor shaft into a different hole in the disc and see if this makes your monster move differently. Try holes at various offset distances and compare the results. Which one makes your monster scuttle most wildly?

★ Try out your brush monster on different surfaces.

★ Swap over the crocodile clips on the back of the motor to see if this affects the direction of movement.

★ Use the dustpan to make a comfy bed for your tired brush monster!

MAKING A SPLASH

SAILING BOAT

Turn a foam pizza disc into a boat to sail across your bath.

YOU WILL NEED:

1 large polystyrene foam pizza disc
25 cm or more in diameter

1 wooden skewer
(cut off the sharp tip)

1 sheet of card
such as the side of a cereal box

1 plastic milk bottle lid

optional - 1 sailor
e.g. small plastic toy
(or you can make your own)

FROM YOUR TOOLBOX:

• ruler • felt-tip pen • large scissors • sharp pencil • poster tack • low melt glue gun • hole punch

⚠ **TAKE CARE** with the sharp pencil.

1 Draw a boat base on your pizza disc and cut it out. Make it roughly as long as the pizza disc and quite wide.

If the base is too narrow, the boat may capsize.

2 Make a hole in the bottle lid (see page 18, step 5) and glue it on. Push the skewer (the mast) through the hole into the base.

Put the mast towards the front so the wind in the sail pulls the boat along.

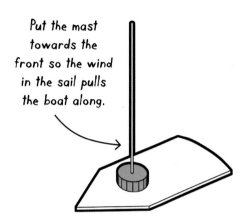

3 Make a card sail slightly shorter than the mast. Punch a hole top and bottom and slide it on. Float your boat on water and blow into the sail.

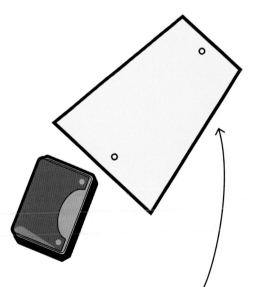

If the sail is narrower at the top, the boat is less likely to fall over when you blow it along.

HOW IT WORKS

This sailing boat design, similar to that used by the ancient Egyptians, only sails in the direction the wind is blowing. Nowadays sailing boats are designed to also sail across the wind.

NOW YOU CAN...

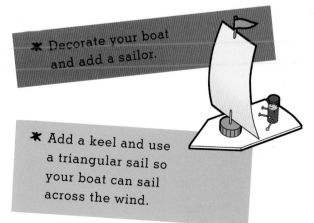

* Decorate your boat and add a sailor.

* Add a keel and use a triangular sail so your boat can sail across the wind.

CARTESIAN DIVER

DIFFICULTY LEVEL ▶▶▶▶ 1

YOU WILL NEED:

1 plastic pipette 5 ml (or 3 ml)

1 M10 nut (M8 nut if using 3 ml pipette)

1 foam craft sheet 2 mm thick

1 small rubber band

1 transparent plastic drinks bottle, easy to squeeze

FROM YOUR TOOLBOX:

• ruler • scissors
• permanent marker pen
• felt-tip pen

Make a diver sink to the bottom of a bottle and rise up again!

DID YOU KNOW?

'Cartesian' comes from the name Descartes. René Descartes was the 17th-century French scientist and mathematician who is said to have invented this experiment.

1 To make the diver, push the nut on to the pipette and cut to the length shown. Draw on a face with permanent marker.

2 Draw this shape on the foam and cut it out. Wrap it around the pipette just below the nut, and hold it in place with a rubber band.

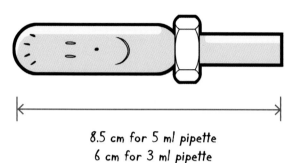

8.5 cm for 5 ml pipette
6 cm for 3 ml pipette

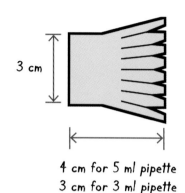

3 cm

4 cm for 5 ml pipette
3 cm for 3 ml pipette

3 Fill the bottle with water, push the diver in and screw on the lid. Squeeze the bottle to make the diver sink. Release it and the diver will rise back to the top!

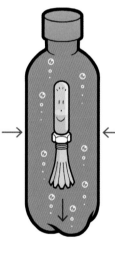

NOW YOU CAN...

* Watch the water level in the pipette rise as you squeeze the bottle and fall again when you release the bottle.

HOW IT WORKS

The diver includes both air, which is light, and a heavy metal nut. In order to float, the diver needs to be lighter than the same amount of water. When you squeeze the bottle, pressure is passed through the water, squashing (compressing) the air in the pipette. This partly fills with water, so the diver becomes heavier and sinks. When you release the bottle the air expands, pushing the water back out, and the diver becomes lighter and rises.

YOU WILL NEED:

50 wooden lolly sticks
(9–12 cm long)

1 low melt glue stick

1 sheet of A3 paper

10 or more tins of food
(about 500 g each)

1 strong cloth
shopping bag

1 length of wood
roughly 4 cm x 4 cm
x 25 cm

2 tables or stools
the same height

Bubble wrap or similar
soft packaging material

FROM YOUR TOOLBOX:

• low melt glue gun • pencil
• 2 plastic rulers

MAKING A SPLASH

LOLLY STICK BRIDGE

Make the strongest lolly stick bridge
you can using just 50 lolly sticks.

⚠ **TAKE CARE** with hot glue – be careful not to burn yourself. Don't let the bag fall on your feet.

THE CHALLENGE...

1. Your bridge has to span a 20-cm-wide 'river'.
2. The middle of the bridge must clear a height of 7 cm above the 'riverbanks'.
3. You can use up to 50 lolly sticks and a single glue stick.
4. You have 10 minutes to design your bridge and one hour to build it!
5. You will then test your bridge until it breaks to find out how strong it is.

Read right to the end of the project before you start.

1 Sketch out a design on paper. You can lay out your lolly sticks to help you.

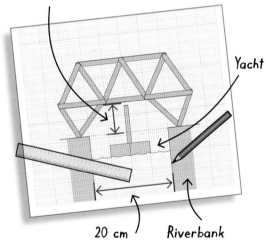

7-cm clearance height

Yacht

20 cm

Riverbank

2 Start building! You might find it easier to work with a friend.

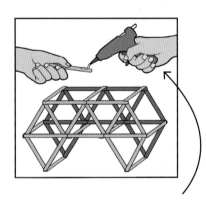

Use a glue gun to stick the lolly sticks together. (PVA glue would take too long to dry.)

3 Position two tables or stools exactly 20 cm apart. Place your bridge across the gap.

Make sure your bridge is long enough to span the 20-cm gap easily.

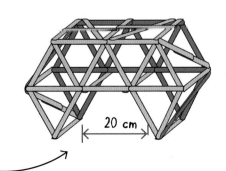

20 cm

4 Place a ruler flat across the gap, then use another ruler to check the clearance height.

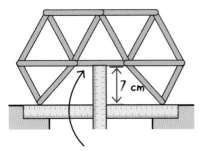

The 7-cm clearance is to the underside of the bridge.

7 cm

 5 Wrap the wood in bubble wrap and place it across the top of the bridge.

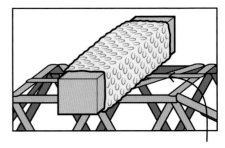

This part of the bridge needs to be flat and strong.

 6 Hang the bag, as shown. Gently place a food tin into the bag. Keep adding tins until the bridge collapses – watch carefully to see how and where it breaks.

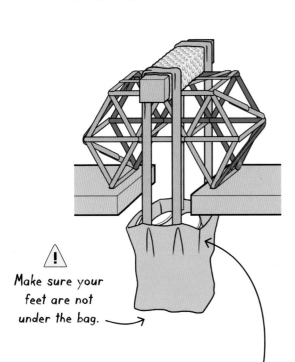

⚠️ *Make sure your feet are not under the bag.* →

The bag must not touch the table or stool legs or the floor as it stretches.

 7 Work out how much load your bridge was able to carry before it collapsed. Count the number of tins in the bag!

1 tin = 0.5 kg
10 tins = 5 kg

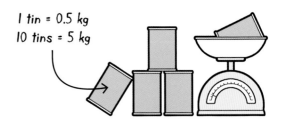

HOW IT WORKS

When you load the middle of your bridge with a heavy weight, the framework transfers the load to the 'banks' on either side that support the bridge. The framework needs to be strong and stable to do this, or the bridge will collapse.

TIPS & HINTS...

1. Your bridge will need to be quite wide so that it doesn't fall over sideways.

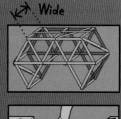

2. Place a ruler flat across the gap between the tables. Push down with your finger (but not too hard) and watch the ruler bend. Now put your ruler on its edge across the gap and push down. You'll see it doesn't bend. If you make your bridge quite thick it should support more load.

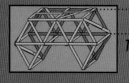

3. Triangle shapes in the bridge framework give it strength because they cannot distort (twist out of shape) in the way that rectangular shapes do when loaded.

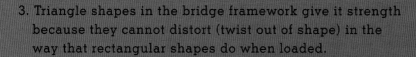

4. If you run out of glue or lolly sticks before your bridge is finished, you can use an extra glue stick or 20 extra lolly sticks, but you will receive a 2 kg weight penalty – your first four cans will not count towards your final score.

NOW YOU CAN...

* Pick up the shopping bag with the tins in to feel how much load your bridge was able to bear.

* From watching your bridge collapse, try to work out which was the weakest part and how you could design a stronger bridge.

* Have a competition with your friends to see who can build the strongest bridge.

MAKING A SPLASH

FAN BOAT

Design an electric fan boat and send it skimming across the water.

⚠ **TAKE CARE** with the propeller – never hold it near your eyes or hair.

1 Using the battery clip, battery holder, crocodile leads, toggle switch, motor and AA cells, follow the steps on pages 8–9 to complete your motor circuit.

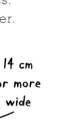

2 Make a card template for the boat base. Use it to cut out two boat shapes from pizza discs. Glue the two shapes together.

3 Decide where to put the motor, battery and switch. The motor can be at the front or back, but keep the boat balanced.

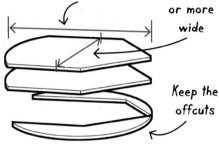

Diameter of disc

14 cm or more wide

Keep the offcuts

The wide shape helps to prevent the boat capsizing.

Motor   Switch   Battery

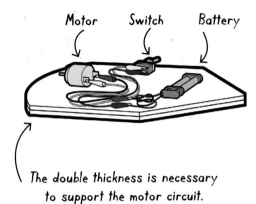

The double thickness is necessary to support the motor circuit.

4 Assemble the motor unit as shown. Check that the propeller won't hit the base. Glue the motor unit to the base.

5 Switch on and check that the propeller turns. If it hits the cotton reels, slide the motor forwards in its mount.

Push propeller onto motor shaft

Glue here

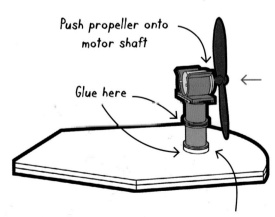

If necessary, raise the propeller by adding discs made from foam offcuts.

Never hold the propeller near your eyes or hair.

Make sure there is a gap between the propeller and cotton reels.

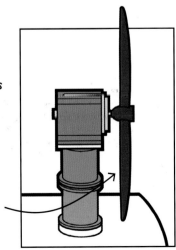

Put the battery unit in a plastic bag to keep it dry. Make it a platform from foam offcuts. Check the boat is balanced, then glue on the battery unit.

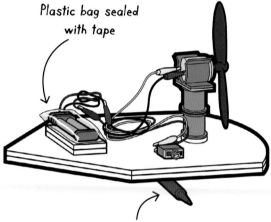

Plastic bag sealed with tape

Rest the boat on a felt-tip pen to check that it is balanced.

 Make the switch a platform from offcuts to keep it dry. Glue the platform to the base and the switch to the platform.

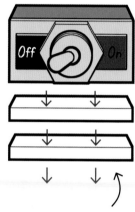

Double platform made from pizza disc offcuts

 Make sure the crocodile leads won't get in the way of the propeller. Fold them up neatly and cable-tie them together.

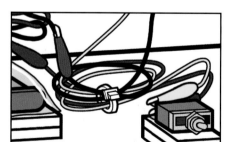

 Try out your fan boat on water – for example in the bath!

If your boat goes backwards, swap over these two crocodile clips to make it go forwards.

HOW IT WORKS

If a material is heavier than the same amount of water then it will sink. Polystyrene foam pizza discs contain lots of bubbles of trapped air. This makes them lighter than water, so they float.

Propeller blades are designed to 'scoop up' air, so the propeller will work better one way round than the other. (Imagine what would happen if you tried to scoop up soup with your spoon upside down!) Look closely at your propeller and see if you can tell which way round it should be mounted.

NOW YOU CAN...

* Try the propeller both ways round. Which goes faster? If you can't turn the propeller round, try turning the whole motor round instead.

* Using pizza disc offcuts, add some fins or a shallow keel to help the boat go in a straight line.

* Try making the boat more streamlined to help it go faster.

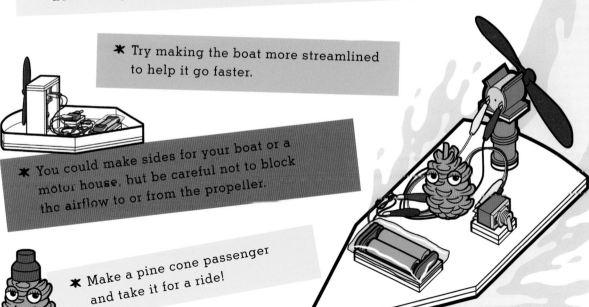

* You could make sides for your boat or a motor house, but be careful not to block the airflow to or from the propeller.

* Make a pine cone passenger and take it for a ride!

SPEEDING THROUGH THE AIR

TEDDY ZIP WIRE

Construct a zip wire and send your teddy whizzing across the room!

YOU WILL NEED:

1 plastic pulley
about 30–50-mm diameter,
4–5-mm central hole

2 old CDs

2 plastic milk bottle lids

1 wooden skewer

1 teddy or similar toy,
weight 50–500 g

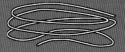

5 m of string

FROM YOUR TOOLBOX:

• sandpaper • low melt glue gun • marker pen • poster tack • pencil sharpener • pencil • large scissors • secateurs • ruler

44

⚠ **TAKE CARE** with the sharp pencil. Only adults should use the secateurs.

1 Using sandpaper, roughen the surface of the CD inner circles. Glue the pulley to these surfaces, lining up the centres.

Don't get glue in the V-shaped groove or central hole of the pulley.

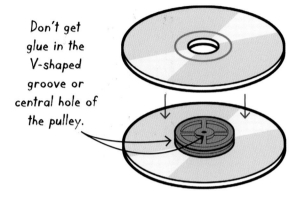

2 Look carefully at the lids. Mark a spot on the outside of each one, between any ridges on the inside or outside, as shown.

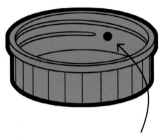

The mark is where you will pierce the lid.

3 ⚠ Push the lid onto a lump of poster tack. Use a sharp pencil to pierce a hole in the side wall. Make a second hole in the top. Repeat with the second lid.

4 Use the scissors to cut off the sharp tip of a wooden skewer. Slightly sharpen the blunt end and slide it through the central hole in the pulley/CD unit.

Both ends should be slightly sharpened but not spiked.

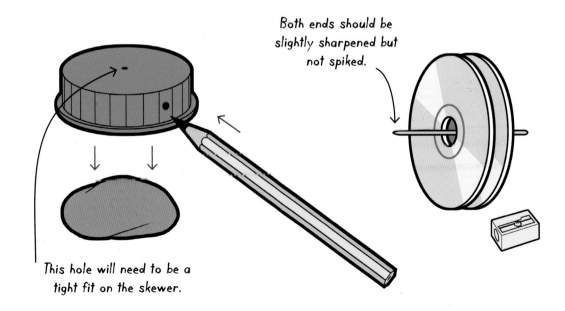

This hole will need to be a tight fit on the skewer.

Slide on the two lids, open ends outwards. Hold the skewer and spin the CD unit to check it rotates freely.

 Rotate the lids so that the holes line up, as shown. Ask an adult to cut off the ends of the skewer with secateurs.

If the pulley doesn't rotate freely, try moving the lids apart slightly.

Leave a small gap.

Holes are lined up.

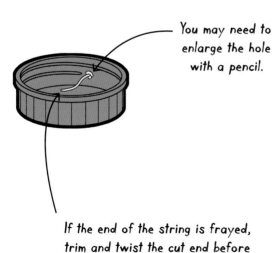 Cut two 40-cm lengths of string. Tie one end of each around your teddy's paws. Push the other ends through the holes in the lids, check the strings are the same length and knot the ends.

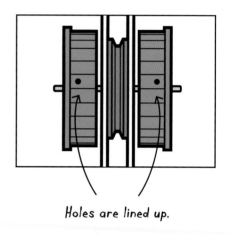 Tie the remaining string to a door handle. Feed the other end under the pulley and hold the end tight. Lower it to make your teddy zip towards you and raise it to make teddy zip away.

You may need to enlarge the hole with a pencil.

If the end of the string is frayed, trim and twist the cut end before pushing it through the hole.

HOW IT WORKS

The teddy travels down the sloping string due to gravity. If the CD/pulley unit with the teddy attached simply slid down the string, there would be high friction and this would make it hard for the pulley to move. However, because the CD/pulley unit is free to rotate, it rolls down the string. This reduces the friction, allowing the teddy to zip down even a shallow slope.

NOW YOU CAN...

* Experiment with the string at different slopes to see what effect this has.

* Try slackening the string a little so that the teddy slows down at the end of the ride instead of crashing.

* Push the bottle lids up against the CD/pulley unit to stop it rotating. How steep a slope do you need now for the teddy to move?

* Set up zip wires around your room or down the stairs – but warn your family first!

* Attach a string to your teddy so that you can pull it back up when it has finished its ride.

* Experiment using teddies of different weights to see which goes fastest.

DIFFICULTY LEVEL ▶▶▶▶ 2

STOMP ROCKET

Make a mobile rocket launcher to send an air-powered rocket high into the sky.

YOU WILL NEED:

1 fizzy drinks bottle (2 litre) without lid

1 plastic milk bottle (4 pint)

1 plastic milk bottle lid

0.7 m clean garden hose

1 clean, straight tube, plastic (preferably) or cardboard 2–3-cm diameter

1 A4 sheet of card

500 g marbles or pebbles 3-cm diameter or less

FROM YOUR TOOLBOX:

• double-sided foam tape
• duct tape • vice • junior hacksaw • sandpaper • marker pen • nail scissors • pencil
• ruler • sticky tape • scissors

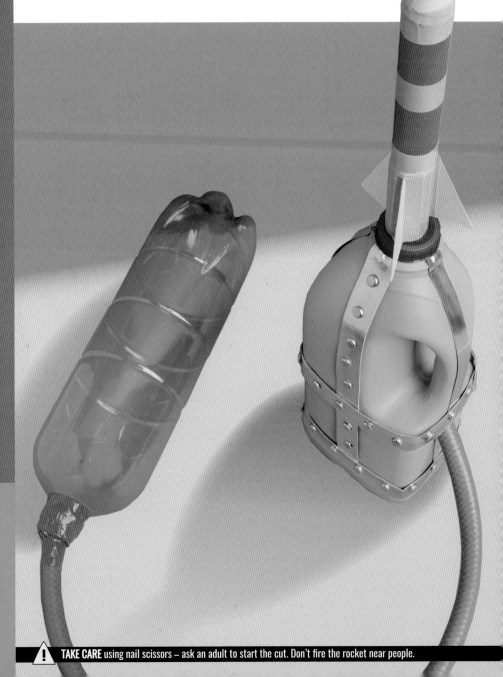

⚠ TAKE CARE using nail scissors – ask an adult to start the cut. Don't fire the rocket near people.

Wrap double-sided foam tape around one end of the hose and push it into the fizzy drinks bottle – it must fit tightly in the neck. Secure with duct tape.

Put the marbles or pebbles into the milk bottle to stop it falling over. Make a hole just below the handle. Push the hose into the hole and out of the bottle neck.

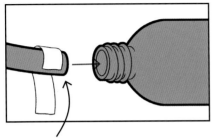

Remove the plastic backing from the foam tape as you wind it so the tape sticks together properly.

Use nail scissors to make the hole - ask an adult to help you.

Clamp the tube gently in the vice and saw off 20 cm. Smooth off the end. Cut a hole in the milk bottle lid the same size as the end of the tube.

To make the card rocket, cut out a 16-cm square of card and roll it around the tube. Put sticky tape around it, as shown, then all the way along the seam.

Draw round the tube end.

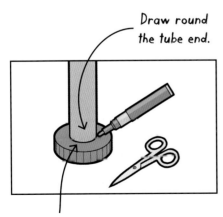

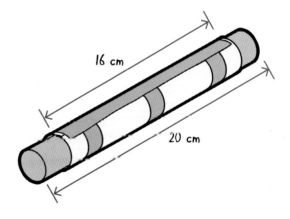

16 cm

20 cm

Cut out the circle with nail scissors. (In step 7 you'll fit the tube into the hole and it will need to be a tight fit.)

The card must be closely wrapped around the tube, but loose enough to slide easily along it.

5 Cut out a card circle and tape it to the end of the rocket. Blow through the tube to check your rocket flies off the tube easily.

Tape on the card circle.

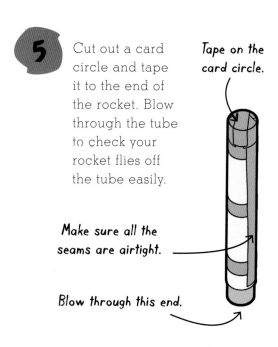

Make sure all the seams are airtight.

Blow through this end.

6 Wrap double-sided foam tape around the end of the hose that's sticking out of the top of the milk bottle and push it into the tube. Secure with duct tape.

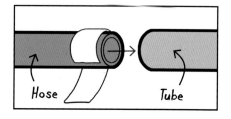

Hose

Tube

Remove the plastic backing from the foam tape as you wind it.

Make sure the seal is airtight.

7 Slide the bottle lid down the tube until it touches the top of the duct tape, then screw it onto the milk bottle. Slide the rocket onto the tube.

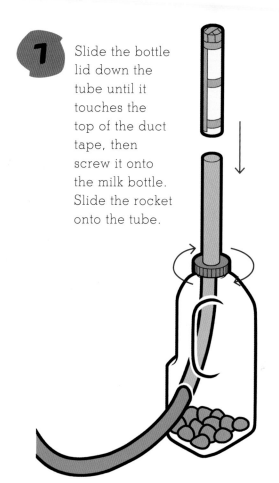

8 Stomp hard on the fizzy drinks bottle to fire the rocket. Blow down the tube to re-charge the bottle with air for your next rocket launch.

⚠ *Don't fire the rocket near people.*

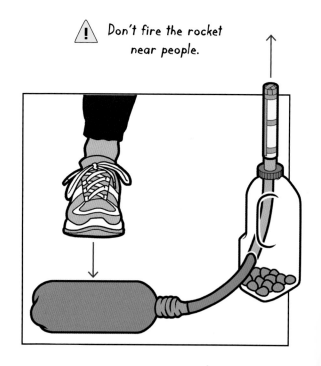

HOW IT WORKS

When you stomp on the fizzy drinks bottle, you force air along the hose and up the tube into the rocket. This pushes the rocket off the end of the tube, allowing the air to escape. If the rocket fits too tightly on the tube, then the friction between them will make it difficult for the rocket to launch. If it is too loose, then air can escape easily down the sides so the rocket won't go as high.

NOW YOU CAN...

* Make a nose cone for your rocket from a semicircle of card. Tape up the seam and attach it to your rocket. The cone should help the rocket to fly straight and make it more streamlined, so it cuts through the air more easily.

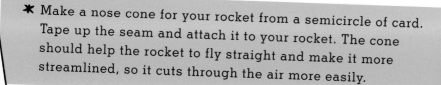

* Make some card fins for your rocket, about 6 cm long. The fins help to stabilize the rocket – they keep it pointing in the direction of travel instead of tumbling through the air.

* Try and get your rocket to go higher by using a larger diameter hose, such as a bicycle inner tube. Using a shorter, wider tube should make it easier for the air to pass through.

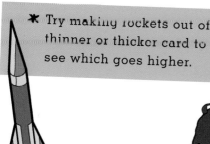

* Try making rockets out of thinner or thicker card to see which goes higher.

SPEEDING THROUGH THE AIR

GLIDER

Make a glider from foam pizza discs and send it soaring across the room.

YOU WILL NEED:

1 photocopy (enlarged 170 per cent) of glider template

2 large polystyrene foam pizza discs 30 cm or more in diameter

Wire paper clips various sizes

FROM YOUR TOOLBOX:

• large scissors • felt-tip pen
• nail scissors • sticky tape
• paints (optional)

⚠ **TAKE CARE** Only adults should use the craft knife.

1 Take a photocopy of the glider template, enlarging it by 170 per cent so that it fits onto one A3 sheet of paper or two A4 sheets.

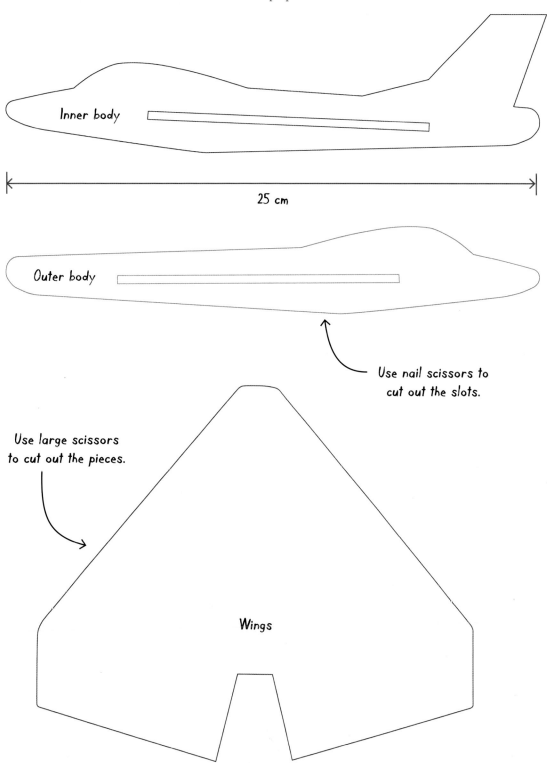

Inner body

25 cm

Outer body

Use nail scissors to cut out the slots.

Use large scissors to cut out the pieces.

Wings

2 If your pizza discs are dimpled on one side, turn them dimpled side down. Place the template parts on the pizza discs and draw round them.

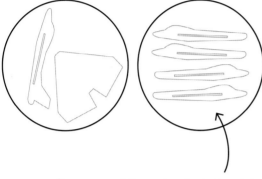

Draw round the outer body template twice one way up, then flip it over and draw round it twice the other way up.

 3 Cut out the parts with large scissors and the slots with nail scissors. Make sure that each slot is big enough for the wing section to slide through.

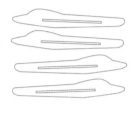

⚠ *Alternatively, ask an adult to cut out the parts using a craft knife.*

 4 Sandwich the body parts together, as shown, then check that the slot in the wings is wide enough for the body to fit into.

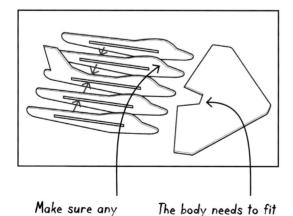

Make sure any dimpled sides face the middle.

The body needs to fit here. Widen the gap if necessary.

 5 Slide the body over one wing until the back of the body fits into the wing slot, as shown. Then slide the front of the body over the front of the wings.

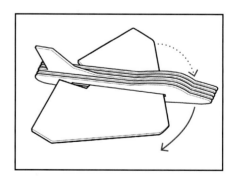

Adjust the body position to make the glider as symmetrical as possible.

Bend a large paper clip to fit closely over the nose. Tape the back of the body parts together.

Attach paper clip like this.

Balance the glider on your finger - it should balance about half way along.

7 Launch your glider as shown, and watch how it flies!

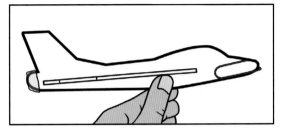

Hold and throw!

NOW YOU CAN...

★ Make improvements! Try to stop the nose of the glider tilting up or down too much by adjusting the size or number of paper clips.

★ Try bending the wings up slightly as shown to make a very shallow V shape – this can help the glider to fly straight.

★ Try bending the back of the wings up very slightly to make the nose of the glider tilt up when in flight. But don't bend too much or the glider will try to climb, slow down and stop flying, or 'stall'.

HOW IT WORKS

Gliders are aircraft without engines. They are relatively lightweight and have large wings that help them to stay up in the air. As the glider travels forward (and slightly downward) through the air, the smooth flow of air under and over the wings creates an upward lift that opposes the downward pull of gravity.

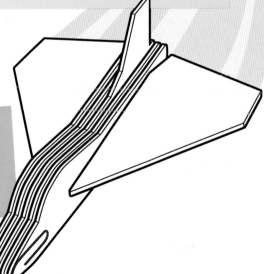

SPEEDING THROUGH THE AIR

CATAPULT

Create your very own ancient siege weapon to bombard the enemy ramparts!

YOU WILL NEED:

Square section wood
12 mm x 12 mm x 1 m long

2 countersunk Pozidriv® screws, 3-mm thread x 15 mm long (size 6 x 5/8")

5 plastic milk bottle lids

2 pieces of wooden skewer 11 cm long

2 pieces of 6-mm-diameter rod x 9 cm long

1 cocktail stick

4 countersunk Pozidriv® screws 3-mm thread x 25 mm long (size 6 x 1")

2 rubber bands – one roughly 1 mm x 4 mm x 16 cm; the other 1 mm x 4mm x 8 cm

Pompom or similar lightweight missile

FROM YOUR TOOLBOX:

• ruler • pencil • junior hacksaw • vice • sandpaper • bradawl • drill with drill bits 2 mm, 2.5 mm, 3.5 mm, 6 mm, 7 mm (a pillar drill would be even better) • Pozidriv® screwdriver • double-sided foam sticky tape • large scissors • masking tape • pencil sharpener • poster tack • hammer • secateurs

⚠ **TAKE CARE** using the saw and drill – ask an adult for help. Take care with the sharp pencil. Only adults should use the secateurs. Only fire lightweight missiles.

THROWING ARM

1 Look at the picture and try to work out what each part of the catapult does. Which parts move and which parts stay still?

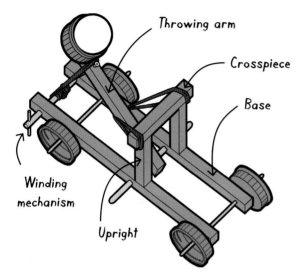

Throwing arm

Crosspiece

Base

Winding mechanism

Upright

2 ⚠ To make the throwing arm, saw off 17 cm of wood. Smooth all the edges with sandpaper. Make two marks, as shown.

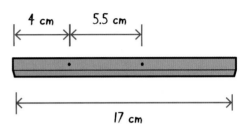

4 cm   5.5 cm

17 cm

To avoid splitting the wood when sawing it, turn it over just before you break through and cut from the other side.

3 ⚠ Indent the two marks, then drill 2.5-mm-diameter holes all the way through. Smooth with sandpaper. Screw in the 15-mm screws, one from the top and one from the bottom, leaving the heads sticking out 4 mm.

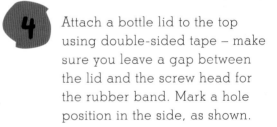

4 mm

Be careful to hold the drill straight or you may snap the drill bit.

4 Attach a bottle lid to the top using double-sided tape – make sure you leave a gap between the lid and the screw head for the rubber band. Mark a hole position in the side, as shown.

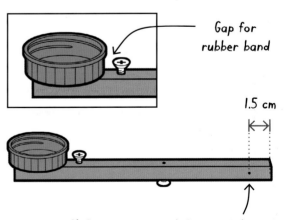

Gap for rubber band

1.5 cm

Make sure the mark for the hole is on the centre-line of the wood.

5 Clamp the wood firmly in the vice to stop it splitting, make an indent on the mark, drill a 2.5-mm pilot hole, then enlarge it to 7 mm. Smooth the wood with sandpaper.

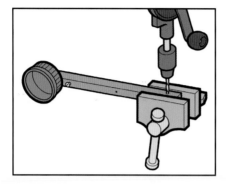

Making an indent helps you to drill in the right place.

BASE

6 For the base, cut two 26-cm lengths of wood. Tape them together with masking tape. Mark, indent and drill four 3.5-mm holes, as shown, through both pieces of wood.

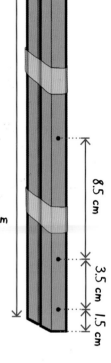

1.5 cm

8.5 cm

3.5 cm 1.5 cm

26 cm

The holes need to stay on the centre line through both pieces of wood, so hold the drill very straight.

7 Mark, indent and drill a 3.5-mm hole in the top of each base piece. (These holes will be used to attach the crosspiece at step 20). Remove the masking tape.

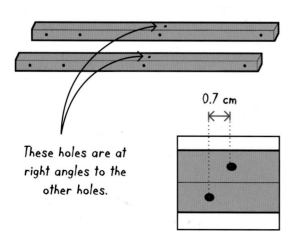

0.7 cm

These holes are at right angles to the other holes.

8 Clamp each piece and enlarge the central hole in the side to 6 mm and the end hole shown to 7 mm. Smooth with sandpaper.

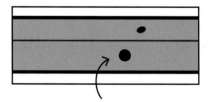

Enlarge the central side holes to 6 mm.

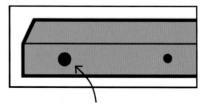

Enlarge the holes at this end to 7 mm.

9 Slightly sharpen the rod and skewer ends. Clamp one part of the base and fit a rod into the central 6-mm hole and the skewers into the 3.5-mm holes.

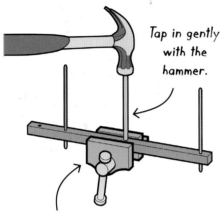

Tap in gently with the hammer.

Clamp the wood below where you are tapping.

10 Slide the throwing arm onto the rod. Push the second side of the base onto the skewers and rod, leaving a gap of 3.8 cm between the base parts.

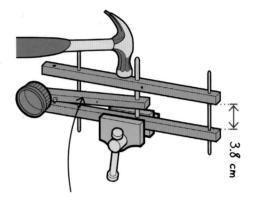

3.8 cm

Make sure you fit the throwing arm the right way round.

WHEELS

11 Make a hole in the centre of the four remaining bottle lids (see page 18, step 5) and push them onto the ends of the skewers with the open ends facing out.

⚠️

Ask an adult to trim off the ends of the skewers with secateurs.

The wheels are not intended to rotate.

WINDING MECHANISM

12 To make the winding mechanism, clamp the remaining rod in the vice. Mark, indent and drill a 2-mm hole right through, 5 mm from the end.

⚠️

5 mm

Be careful to hold the drill straight or you may snap the drill bit.

13 Mark, indent and drill another 2-mm hole at the other end, but make this hole roughly at right angles to the first hole, as shown. Smooth with sandpaper.

⚠

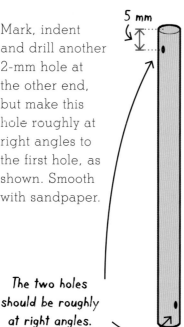

5 mm

The two holes should be roughly at right angles.

14 Slide the rod into the 7-mm holes in the base and make sure it rotates easily.

⚠

If the rod doesn't turn easily, run the 7-mm drill through the holes again.

15 Use the scissors to snip the tips off a cocktail stick, then cut it in half. Tap the pieces gently into the 2-mm holes so they stick out an equal length on both sides.

If the cocktail sticks touch the bottle lids, trim them shorter.

UPRIGHTS

16 Wrap a piece of masking tape around the 2.5-mm drill bit, 1.5 cm from its tip. This will help you to drill the right depth hole in the uprights (see step 17).

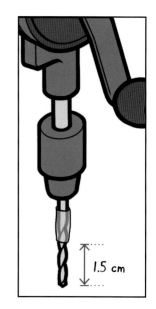

When the masking tape touches the wood, you'll know your hole is the right depth.

1.5 cm

17 For the uprights, cut and sand two 4.5-cm lengths of square section wood. Clamp as shown, then indent and drill a 2.5-mm-diameter hole at each end, 1.5 cm deep.

CROSSPIECE

18 To make the crosspiece, cut an 8-cm length of square section wood and mark, indent and drill two 3.5-mm-diameter holes, as shown.

Hold the drill straight and drill in the middle of the wood.

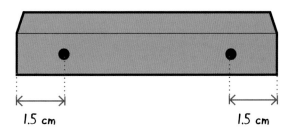

1.5 cm   1.5 cm

Smooth all sides and edges so that they won't damage the rubber band.

19 Tightly screw two 25-mm-long screws through the holes in the crosspiece and into the holes in the uprights, as shown. Remove from the vice.

20 Clamp the crosspiece upside down. Holding the throwing arm against the winding mechanism, screw the base tightly to the crosspiece uprights, as shown, using the holes drilled at step 7.

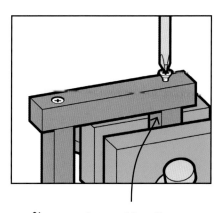

Clamp each upright in the vice before you screw into it.

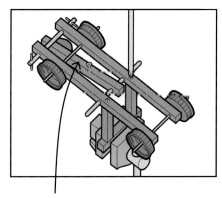

Make sure the throwing arm is at the winding mechanism end.

FIRING MECHANISM

 21 Pass the 8-cm-long rubber band under the throwing arm and hook it over the ends of the crosspiece, as shown.

 22 Loop the 16-cm-long rubber band (or two shorter rubber bands looped together) around the winding mechanism.

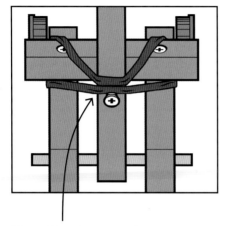

The rubber band should sit just above the screw head.

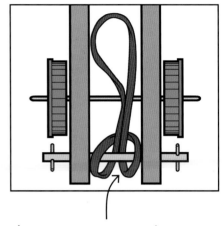

Loop it this way round. If you loop it the other way, it slips.

 23 Pull the rubber band tight around the rod so it doesn't slip when winding up. Hook it over the throwing arm between the bottle lid and screw head.

 24 ⚠ Wind the arm back to prime your catapult and place a missile in the lid, as shown. To fire, let go of the winding mechanism abruptly.

Hook the rubber band just above the screw head.

Take aim and FIRE!

Wind here by turning the cocktail sticks.

HOW IT WORKS

When you wind back the throwing arm, elastic potential energy is stored in the stretched rubber band, which will pull the arm forwards. When you let go, much of this energy is converted to kinetic (movement) energy of the arm and the missile, while some is converted to heat and sound. The throwing arm and missile move together until the arm hits the crosspiece and stops, while the missile carries on.

NOW YOU CAN...

Ping pong ball

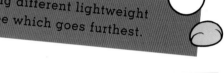

✱ Try catapulting different lightweight missiles to see which goes furthest.

✱ Fit different rubber bands to try and improve performance.

✱ Try holding the base still as you fire to stop the catapult moving – see if this makes the missile go further.

✱ Raise the front of the base up, for example on a book, to see what effect it has.

✱ Try using a deeper bottle lid on the throwing arm.

✱ Invite your friends round to make catapults and hold a competition to see who can fire the furthest.

HANDY AT HOME

CLOCKS

Make either a colourful fuse bead clock or a sturdy grandfather clock!

YOU WILL NEED:

1 sheet of A4 paper

1 quartz clock analogue movement module with mount and threaded spindle

1 M8 x 25 mm 'penny' (repair) washer

1 AA cell

For the fused bead clock:

Fuse beads, 5 mm

Large, round pegboard for 5-mm fuse beads

For the grandfather clock:

1 old CD

1 sheet of A3 paper

1 sheet of A3 card roughly 1.2 mm thick

Optional – number stickers or transfers

FROM YOUR TOOLBOX:

• pencil • ruler • protractor or 30º set square • greaseproof paper • iron and ironing board • permanent marker pen • large scissors • paint • paintbrush • low melt glue gun

⚠ **TAKE CARE** using the iron – ask an adult for help.

NUMBER GUIDE FOR BOTH CLOCKS...

 Draw a large cross on a sheet of A4 paper. Make sure the lines cross at 90°. Divide each quarter into three, as shown. Label the lines 1 to 12.

 Measure the diameter of your CD or pegboard. Halve the number to find the radius and mark this distance from the centre on the guide lines.

Use the 30° set square or protractor to mark out lines at intervals of 30° around the circle.

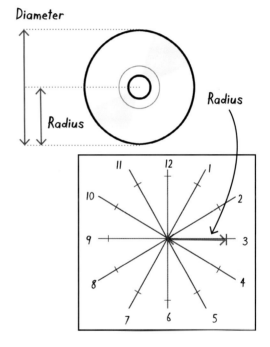

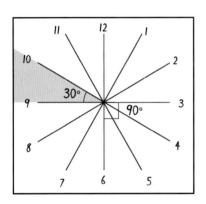

 Use the marks on the lines to help you place your CD or pegboard exactly over the central cross, as shown

These lines will help you to position the numbers on your clock face.

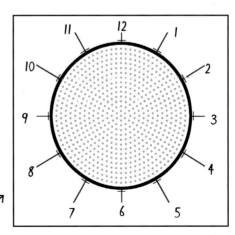

TO MAKE A FUSED BEAD CLOCK...

 4 Design a clock face on your pegboard, leaving out the central peg and first circle of pegs. Use your number guide to help you position the numbers.

 5 Cover with greaseproof paper and iron. When you think the beads have fused, lift a corner of the paper. If any beads come loose, replace and iron again.

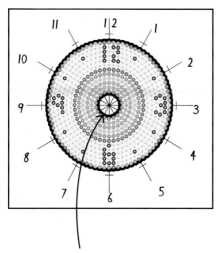

Remember to leave a hole to fit over the clock spindle.

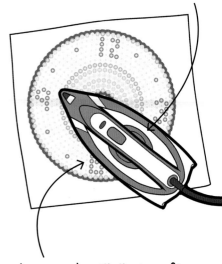

Iron at just below medium setting.

Press down evenly with the iron. Stop ironing when the beads have fused together.

 6 Place some heavy books on top of the paper while the clock face cools. When cool, take the clock face off the pegboard, turn it over, cover with greaseproof paper and iron again.

The heavy books stop the clock face distorting as it cools.

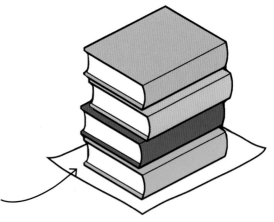

TO MAKE A GRANDFATHER CLOCK...

 Using your number guide, write the numbers 1 to 12 on your CD using permanent pen, or attach number stickers or transfers.

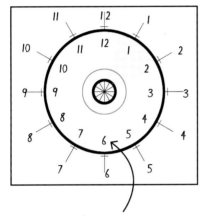

Make sure the numbers line up with the ones on the guide you made.

 Design your grandfather clock on A3 paper. Work out where the clock face will go and mark the centre.

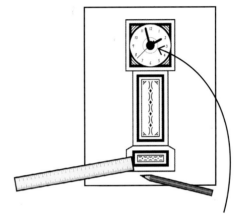

The mark in the centre shows where the spindle will go.

 Transfer your design onto A3 card – you could use your paper design as a template. Cut out the card parts.

Make a hole in the centre of the clock face.

 Paint the parts, wait for them to dry, then draw on extra features. Glue the parts together.

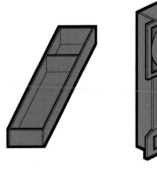

If the card curves as it dries, paint the other side to help straighten it out.

ASSEMBLING YOUR CLOCK...

1 Take the clock movement module and place the mounting bracket over the spindle.

Mounting bracket

Spindle

Clock movement module

2 Fit the rubber washer.

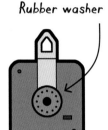

Rubber washer

3 For the grandfather clock, push the spindle through the hole in the card from behind.

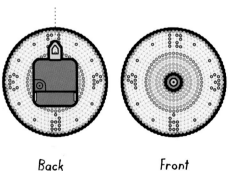

Back of clock face

4 Place the clock face over the spindle, as shown.

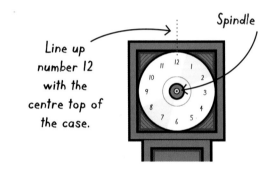

Spindle

Line up number 12 with the centre top of the case.

5 For the fused bead clock, line up number 12 with the mounting bracket on the back.

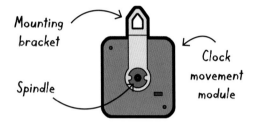

Back   Front

6 On your chosen clock, fit the M8 x 25 mm 'penny' washer on the front.

M8 x 25 mm 'penny' washer

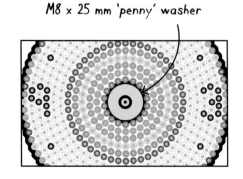

7 Screw down the nut, making sure the clock face and washer are central on the spindle.

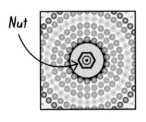

Nut

If the spindle is too short, fit the rubber washer instead of the 'penny' washer.

8 Push on the short hour hand, the medium-length minute hand and lastly the second hand.

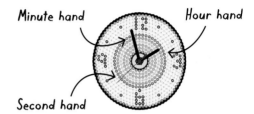

Minute hand

Hour hand

Second hand

9 Fit the AA cell into the slot in the case. Make sure the second hand goes round, and set the correct time. Your clock is ready!

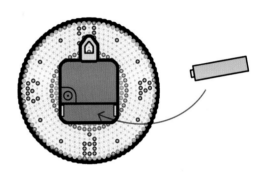

HOW IT WORKS

The movement module contains a circuit with a tiny crystal that vibrates at a very precise rate. The circuit counts these vibrations and uses this information to send out a pulse of electricity once a second to turn a tiny motor. This motor turns the gears, which drive the clock hands round at different speeds.

NOW YOU CAN...

* Find the best place in your bedroom for your cool clock!

HANDHELD FAN

Stay cool with this handheld fan made from a plastic drinks bottle.

YOU WILL NEED:

For the circuit:
• 1 battery clip • 1 battery holder • 3 crocodile leads
• 1 toggle switch • 1 motor
• 2 AA cells

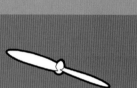

1 propeller
about 15-cm diameter with hole all the way through (must be tight fit on 2-mm-diameter motor shaft)

1 plastic drinks bottle (neck wide enough for motor to fit inside)

1 small rubber band
2–5 cm long

FROM YOUR TOOLBOX:

• nail scissors • ruler
• double-sided foam sticky tape • sticky tape

⚠ **TAKE CARE** with the propeller – never hold it near eyes or hair. Take care using nail scissors – ask an adult to start the cut.

1 Using the battery clip, battery holder, crocodile leads, toggle switch, motor and AA cells, follow the steps on pages 8–9 to complete your motor circuit.

2 ⚠ Press the propeller onto the motor shaft. Hold the motor facing upwards, switch on and check the propeller goes round.

3 The air should blow upwards. If it blows downwards, swap over the crocodile clips attached to the motor.

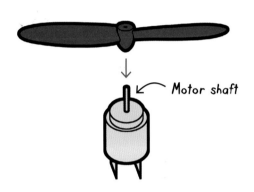

Motor shaft

4 Using the nail scissors, cut the bottle carefully in two. If the bottle has a waist, cut it slightly above the narrowest point.

5 Neatly trim the edge of the lower part of the bottle. Trim about 1 cm off the top part so it will fit snugly onto the lower part.

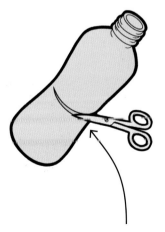

⚠ *Ask an adult to start the cut for you.*

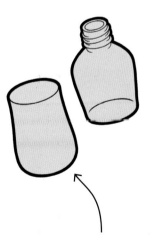

If wet, dry the inside of the bottle with kitchen paper.

Stretch the rubber band over the crocodile clips and switch, as shown. Make sure it goes under the on/off label.

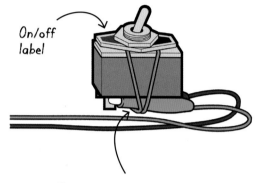

On/off label

The rubber band will stop the crocodile clips coming off when you fit the switch to the bottle.

 Ask an adult to help you cut a 1.2-cm-diameter hole in the bottle to mount your switch. It needs to fit tightly.

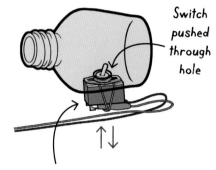

Switch pushed through hole

Push the switch in from the outside just to check that the hole is big enough, then take it out again.

 Unclip the crocodile clips from the motor, push them up through the neck of the bottle, then re-connect them.

Switch on and make sure the propeller still blows air upwards.

 Wind foam tape around the motor, remove the plastic backing and push the motor down into the bottle neck as shown. It should fit tightly.

For a narrow neck put foam tape part way round. For a wide neck you'll need several layers.

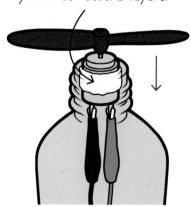

10 Remove the switch's nut and on/off label. Push the cylindrical part through the hole from the inside, refit the label and screw the nut down firmly.

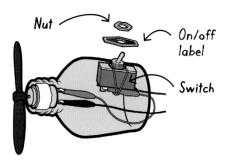

Nut

On/off label

Switch

11 Place the battery in the bottom of the bottle. Push the crocodile leads in. Slide the two parts of the bottle together and secure with tape.

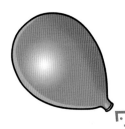

Be careful not to touch bare metal parts together and cause a short circuit.

12 Try out your fan with the propeller either way up.

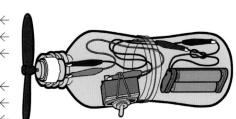

NOW YOU CAN...

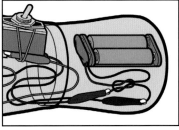

HOW IT WORKS

As it turns, the propeller produces a stream of air. The blades are set at an angle, pushing air upwards. If you connect the motor the other way, the propeller will move in the opposite direction and push air downwards.

Air pushed this way

Propeller turns clockwise

✱ Use your fan to keep balloons in the air! Move them around the room by directing the air stream at them.

HANDY AT HOME

TORCH

Make a torch in a bottle and explore coloured light and shadows.

⚠ **TAKE CARE** using nail scissors – ask an adult to start the cut. Watch out for sharp metal edges.

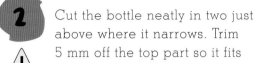 Using the battery clip, battery holder, crocodile leads, toggle switch, bulb, bulb holder and AA cells, follow the steps on pages 8–9 to complete the bulb circuit.

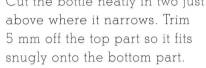 Cut the bottle neatly in two just above where it narrows. Trim 5 mm off the top part so it fits snugly onto the bottom part.

 Ask an adult to help you cut a 1.2-cm-diameter hole for the switch in the position shown.

Ask an adult to start the cut for you.

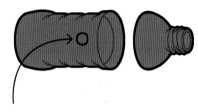

The hole will need to be a tight fit on the cylindrical part of the switch.

To make the foil reflector, start by measuring the length of the bottleneck and the inside diameter, as shown.

 Draw a rectangle on the aluminium foil, as shown. Cut it out, roll it into a cylinder and push it into the bottleneck. Watch out for sharp edges.

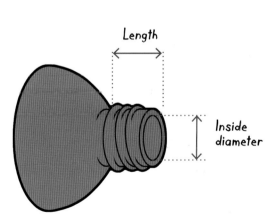

Length

Inside diameter

3 x inside diameter of bollleneck

Length of bottleneck

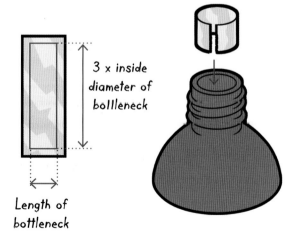

6 Stick double-sided foam tape over the screws, then push the bulb holder up into the bottle. The screws mustn't touch the reflector and cause a short circuit (see page 119).

7 Stretch the rubber band over the switch and crocodile clips, as shown. Fit the switch (see page 73, step 10). Switch on to check that the bulb lights up.

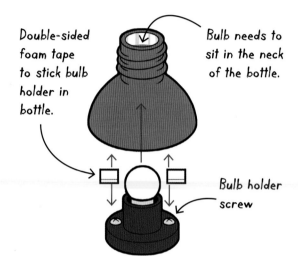

Double-sided foam tape to stick bulb holder in bottle.

Bulb needs to sit in the neck of the bottle.

Bulb holder screw

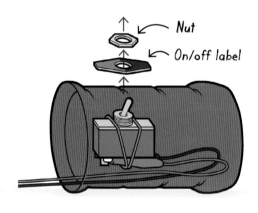

Nut

On/off label

If the nut comes loose during use, tighten it up again.

8 Put the battery unit and crocodile leads in and tape the two bottle parts together. Use transparent sticky tape to stick a transparent plastic disc over the neck end.

9 Find a dark space and have fun trying out your torch!

To fix any problems, just peel off the tape and open up the bottle.

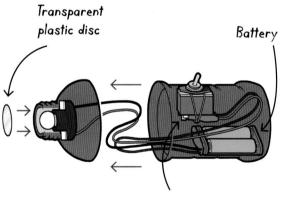

Transparent plastic disc

Battery

Be careful not to touch bare metal parts together when assembling.

HOW IT WORKS

When you switch on the torch, chemical energy stored in the battery is changed into electrical energy, which passes through the bulb. The bulb contains a very thin wire called a filament. The electricity has to work hard to pass through the thin wire, which gets very hot and glows brightly, giving off light and heat energy. The filament is made of a metal such as tungsten, which has a high melting temperature. However, if the filament gets too hot it melts, and we say the bulb has 'blown'.

NOW YOU CAN...

★ Work out which of the materials you used reflects light, which allows light to pass through and which stops light.

★ Make coloured light by attaching filters – you could use see-through coloured sweet wrappers held on with rubber bands. Shine different colours onto coloured objects to see what happens. For example, what colour does a green object appear to be in red light?

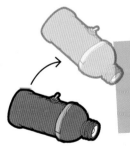

★ In a dark room, ask a friend to hold a felt-tip pen vertically on the floor. Hold your torch above it and move it as though it is the Sun moving across the sky. How does the length of the pen's shadow change?

MAKING LIGHT WORK!

COIN BATTERY

Light up an LED using electricity from a home-made battery!

YOU WILL NEED:

6 copper coins
about 25-mm diameter
e.g. 2p pieces

6 zinc-coated M6 or M8
x 25–30 mm 'penny' (repair)
washers (or 6 discs of
aluminium foil)

1 piece of felt

Vinegar in a glass

1 LED 2V
standard, 5-mm diameter

FROM YOUR TOOLBOX:

• felt-tip pen • scissors
• sticky tape

1 Draw round a coin on the felt. Cut out the disc, soak it in vinegar and place it on top of a washer. Put a coin on top of the felt disc. Repeat five more times.

2 Bend the legs of the LED as shown, so they will fit tightly over the top and bottom of the stack.

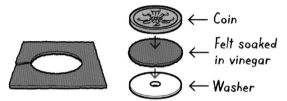

← Coin

← Felt soaked in vinegar

← Washer

Washers are placed directly on top of coins.

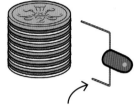

Be careful not to break the legs off when you bend them.

3 Fit the LED to the stack so the longer leg is on the top coin and the shorter leg is on the bottom washer. Hold it on tightly and the LED should light up!

4 Wrap the stack tightly in sticky tape to hold the legs firmly against the coin and washer. This also helps to stop the vinegar drying out.

Unlike bulbs, LEDs only pass current in one direction. If the LED doesn't light up, try it the other way up.

The stack is acting as a battery.

NOW YOU CAN...

✱ Try changing the size of the stack to see if the LED glows more or less brightly.

✱ See how long the LED stays lit, then take the stack apart. The coins and washers will have discoloured where a chemical reaction took place, producing the electric current.

HOW IT WORKS

When the copper in the coin and zinc in the washer react with the vinegar, negative electrical charge builds up on the zinc washer and positive electrical charge on the copper coin. Connecting the LED across the stack completes the circuit so the electricity flows around it, lighting up the LED.

MAKING LIGHT WORK!

COLOURED SPINNER

Experiment with colour blending by making a spinning coloured disc.

YOU WILL NEED:

1 plastic tube with lid fitted roughly 2.5-cm inside diameter x 14 cm long

String
55 cm long

1 wooden rod
6-mm diameter

1 cork
preferably plastic

2 old CDs or DVDs

1 sheet of thick card
about 1.2 mm thick

1 A4 sheet of thin
white card

FROM YOUR TOOLBOX:

• ruler • marker pen • pencil
• vice • drill with 3- & 6-mm-
diameter drill bits
• sandpaper • large scissors
• junior hacksaw • pencil
sharpener • low melt glue
gun • pair of compasses
• coloured felt-tip pens
• double-sided tape

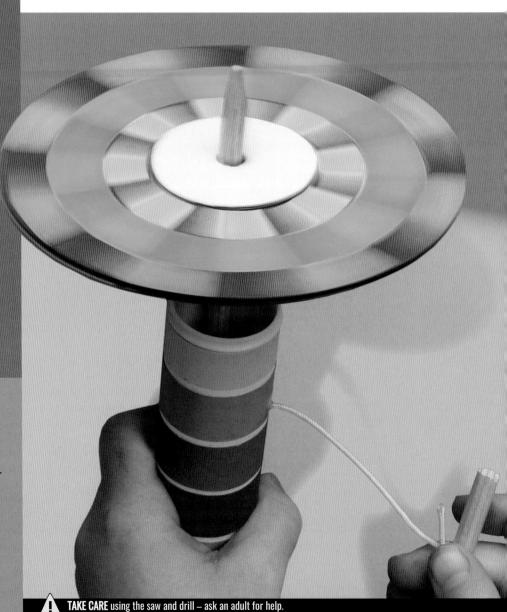

⚠ **TAKE CARE** using the saw and drill – ask an adult for help.

Gently clamp the tube in the vice and drill a 6-mm hole 3 cm from the lid end. Remove the lid and smooth the hole with sandpaper inside and out.

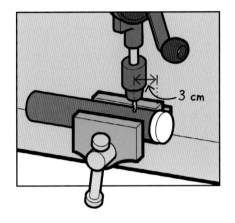

You can support the tube with wood so it doesn't move when you drill it.

 Saw off 21 cm of rod. Saw a small notch 8 cm from one end. Saw off a separate 5-cm length to make a handle and cut a small notch in the middle.

Notch

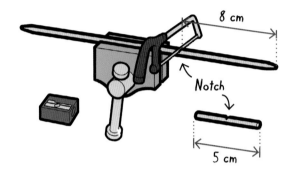

Sharpen the ends of the rod slightly. Smooth both pieces with sandpaper.

 Slide the rod into the tube, notched end first. Saw the cork in half. Drill a 3-mm pilot hole through one half, then enlarge it to 6 mm. Push the half cork onto the rod until it is 1 cm above the rim, as shown.

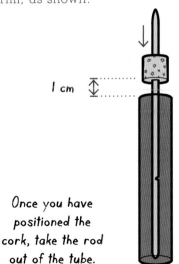

1 cm

Once you have positioned the cork, take the rod out of the tube.

 Glue the two CDs together, then glue them to the top of the cork, lining up the hole centres. Cut a 4-cm-wide disc of thick card and drill a 6-mm hole through it. Put glue on the CD inner circle and cork top, then push the card disc down firmly onto the glue before it cools.

Before gluing, push the card disc onto the rod to make sure it fits, then remove it.

Glue here.

Tie a slip knot in one end of the string and loop it over the notch in the handle. Slide the other end into the hole in the tube, as shown. Tie another slip knot and loop it over the notch in the rod.

 Slide the rod back into the plastic tube. Pull the handle until all the loose string is hanging out. Turn the CD unit to wind in the string.

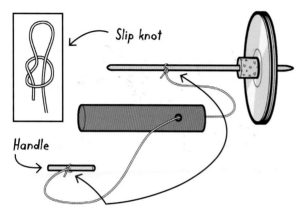

Slip knot

Handle

Pull the string hard to tighten the knots. Try to jam it in the notches so it can't come loose.

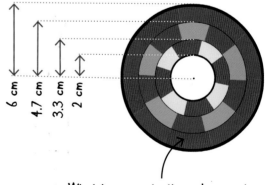

 Hold the tube and pull the handle to spin the CD unit. Just before the string is fully out, leave it slack so it winds back in.

Draw a 6-cm-radius disc on white card. Draw three inner circles, as shown. Cut out the disc and centre circle. Colour the rings with repeating colours. Tape it to the top of the CD unit and spin!

Pull the string again to make the unit spin the other way, then repeat.

6 cm 4.7 cm 3.3 cm 2 cm

What happens to the colours when you spin the disc?

NOW YOU CAN...

* Colour some more card discs in different colours and try them out on the spinner. It's possible to get three discs from one A4 sheet of card.

* Make a Newton disc, named after the 17th-century British scientist Sir Isaac Newton, who invented it. Colour it with the colours of the rainbow. A rainbow is caused by raindrops splitting white light from the Sun into its separate colours, so if you mix light from all the colours of the rainbow you should get white – or nearly white!

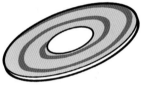

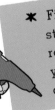

* Fix your spinner! If the string comes loose on the rod, tighten it back up. If your CD unit comes loose, glue it back on.

HOW IT WORKS

Pulling the string makes the CD unit spin and gives it kinetic (movement) energy. When you stop pulling, the energy in the CD unit makes it carry on turning, winding the string back in again. Sharpening the bottom of the rod allows it to spin more easily. If the coloured circles move fast enough, the colours appear to mix together and produce different colours. For example, red and yellow mix to make orange, and blue and red make purple. On a television screen, red, green and blue light are mixed in different amounts to make all the other colours.

MAKING LIGHT WORK!

PERISCOPE

Use mirrors to see around corners and spy on your friends and family!

YOU WILL NEED:

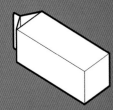

2 rectangular juice cartons about 7 cm x 7 cm x 23 cm

2 mirrors about 6 cm x 6 cm

Thick card about 1.2 mm thick

FROM YOUR TOOLBOX:

• nail scissors • ruler • marker pen • sticky tape • protractor or 45° set square • large scissors • low melt glue gun • plastic bottle lid (3-cm diameter)

⚠ **TAKE CARE** using nail scissors – ask an adult to start the cut. Watch out for sharp mirror edges. Never look directly at the Sun – you could damage your eyes.

1 ⚠️ Use nail scissors to cut the tops neatly off the two cartons. Cut four 2-cm-long slits at the end of one carton. Slot the two cartons together and tape around the join.

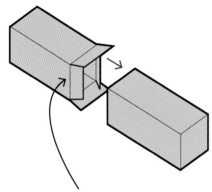

Bend two flaps in slightly and the other two out.

2 Mark a 45° line at both ends of the box, as shown. Turn the box over and mark two more lines running in the same direction.

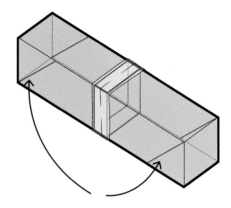

Make sure these lines are facing the lines on the other side.

3 ⚠️ Cut out two 8-cm squares of thick card with the large scissors. Using the nail scissors, cut slits along the 45° lines on the periscope box.

Make each slit just long and wide enough for one of the card squares to slide right through.

4 Glue the mirrors to the cards. Slide the cards in until the mirrors just touch the box. On the box, draw round the bottom of each mirror. Cut along these lines to enlarge the slits.

⚠️
Watch out for sharp edges.

Draw here.

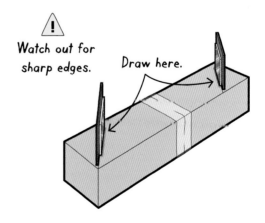

Make sure you stick the mirrors in the centre of the card squares.

5 Slide the mirror units into the box so a little bit of card sticks out on both sides. Tape over the edges of the card, as shown.

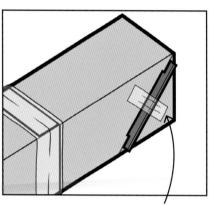

The tape stops the mirror units from sliding out.

 6 Draw round a bottle lid at the position shown and cut out the circle with nail scissors.

3.5 cm

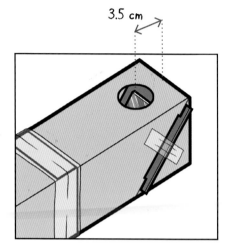

The hole must be facing one of the mirrors.

7 Turn the box over and cut out a rectangular hole at the opposite end, as shown.

1.5 cm
4 cm
5 cm

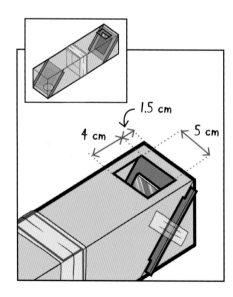

The rectangle must be facing the second mirror.

8 Take a look through the round hole and see what's going on over the wall!

Light rays are reflected down the middle of the box and into your eye.

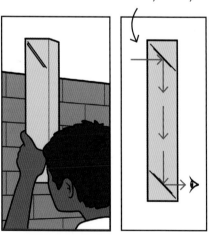

⚠ *Never look at the Sun - you could damage your eyes.*

NOW YOU CAN...

★ Try out your periscope in a crowd to see over people's heads.

★ Use your periscope to spy round doorways or through windows without being seen.

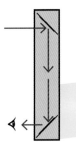

★ Try making a periscope that will show you what's going on behind you.

HOW IT WORKS

Rays of light travel in straight lines. When they hit an object, they bounce off – this is called reflection. Mirrors are smooth and shiny so they reflect light well.

Light rays reflect off a mirror at the same angle as they hit it. Your top mirror is angled at 45° to the incoming light rays, so the rays are reflected down the middle of the periscope box. They then hit the bottom mirror at 45° and are reflected into your eye.

Periscopes were used by soldiers in the First World War to see out of the trenches. Nowadays, they are used in tanks so the people inside can look out without leaving the safety of the tank. On submarines they are used to see what's happening above the water without the vessel having to surface. Periscopes are also used for seeing over the heads of crowds, for example at golf tournaments.

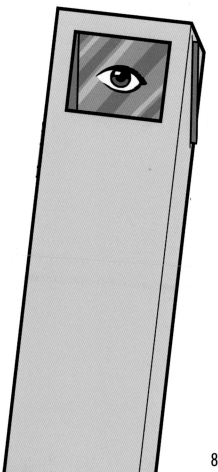

STEADY HAND GAME

Who has the steadiest hand? Design and build a challenging game to find out!

YOU WILL NEED:

For the circuit:
• 1 battery clip • 1 battery holder • 4 crocodile leads
• 1 toggle switch • 1 bulb
• 1 bulb holder • 2 AA cells

1 board e.g. hardboard, MDF, plywood or plastic roughly 3 mm thick x 25 cm x 25 cm

1 bare aluminium wire 2–3-mm diameter (not plastic coated)

1 cork

1 cable tie

FROM YOUR TOOLBOX:

• pencil • vice • hand drill with 4-mm drill bit • sandpaper
• tape measure • wire cutters
• pliers • low melt glue gun

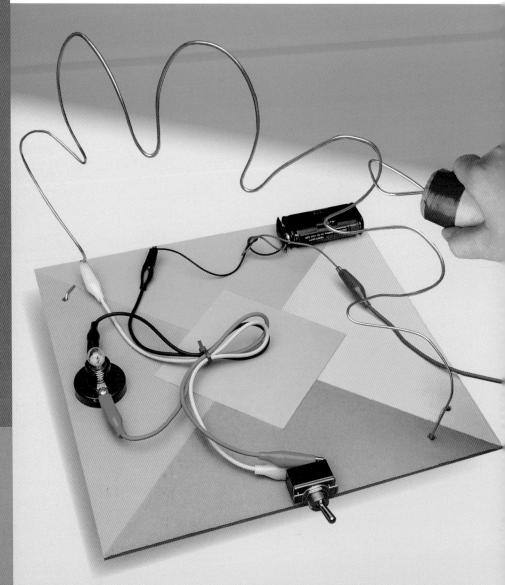

⚠ **TAKE CARE** using the drill – ask an adult for help.

AIM OF THE GAME...

The aim is to move the wire loop from one end of the wire shape to the other without making the bulb light up!

 Using the battery clip, battery holder, three of your four crocodile leads, toggle switch, bulb, bulb holder and AA cells, follow the steps on pages 8–9 to complete the bulb circuit.

 Mark two pairs of holes in opposite corners of the board. Clamp the board in the vice to drill them, as shown.

 Cut 1.2 m of wire. Feed an end down through a hole and back up through the hole next to it, keeping it flat along the bottom.

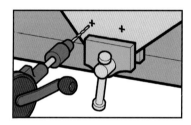

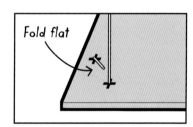

Fold flat

Bend the rest of the wire into your chosen shape. Leave the last 8 cm of wire straight.

 Slide the straight end down through one hole and back up through the hole next to it, as described in step 3.

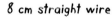
8 cm straight wire

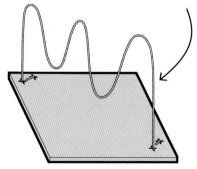

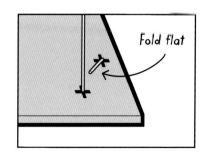
Fold flat

Clamp the cork in the vice. Make an indent in the end with a pencil, then drill a hole all the way through, as shown.

 Cut 16 cm of wire. Loop it around your wire shape, then push one end right through the hole in the cork.

The indent stops the drill bit from wandering and making the hole off-centre.

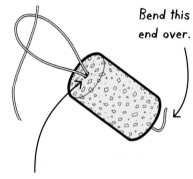

Bend this end over.

Tuck the loose end into the hole.

 Decide where to place the bulb, switch and battery. Glue them on, then switch on to check that the bulb still lights up.

 Disconnect the crocodile clip attached to the red wire from the battery clip, and clip it onto one end of the wire shape.

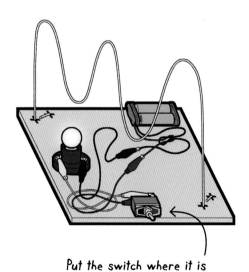

Put the switch where it is easy to reach.

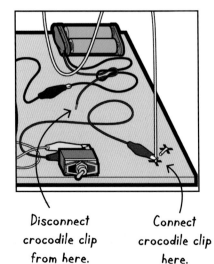

Disconnect crocodile clip from here.

Connect crocodile clip here.

10 Clip the fourth (spare) crocodile lead to the red wire from the battery clip and the wire sticking out of the cork, as shown.

11 Switch on and touch the wire shape with the wire loop to make sure the bulb lights up. Now try out your steady hand game!

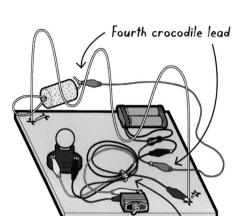

Fourth crocodile lead

Put a cable tie around all the wires except the one attached to the wire loop.

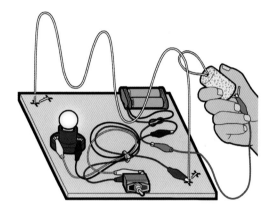

Switch off when not in use.

HOW IT WORKS

With the circuit switched on, the wire shape and wire loop together act like a second switch. When they are in contact this completes the circuit, so the bulb comes on. If not in contact, there is a gap in the circuit and the bulb goes off.

NOW YOU CAN...

* Adjust the wire shape or the size of the wire loop to make the game easier or harder. Make it difficult, but not too difficult to complete.

* Challenge your friends to a steady-hand-game contest!

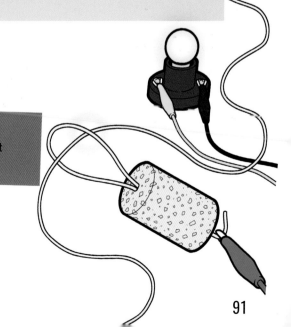

YOU WILL NEED:

1 wooden rod
10.5 cm long to fit pulley

1 base e.g. plywood or MDF
3 mm thick x 6 cm x 16 cm

1 pulley (see page 44)

1 piece of wood
about 1 cm x 3 cm x 10 cm

1 rubber band
1 mm x 1.5 mm x 8–10 cm

3 pop rivets, 3.2-mm
diameter x 6.4 mm

1 stiff plastic tube or straw
5-mm diameter x 7 cm long

1 motor pulley, tight fit on
2-mm-diameter motor shaft,
overall diameter 7.5 mm,
pulley inner diameter 3 mm

1 thin plastic tube 2-mm
inside diameter x 6 cm long

1 white bead (Moon), about
8-mm diameter, 3.5-mm hole

1 wooden skewer, 5 cm length

2 polystyrene balls (Earth and
Sun) 1-cm & 4-cm diameter

FROM YOUR TOOLBOX:

• pencil sharpener • ruler
• pencil • vice • drill, 3.2- &
5-mm drill bits & drill bit same
diameter as rod • sandpaper
• junior hacksaw • low melt glue
gun • plastic bottle lid 3 cm
diameter • wood file
• paintbrush • acrylic paints

MAKING LIGHT WORK!

ORBITING IN SPACE

Make a moving model of Earth orbiting the Sun while the Moon orbits Earth.

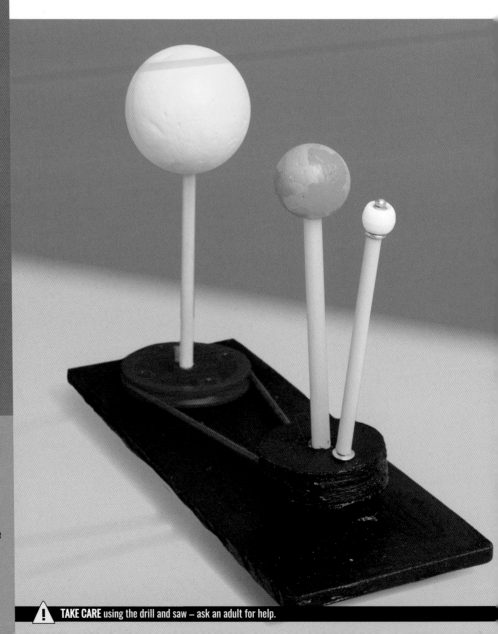

⚠ **TAKE CARE** using the drill and saw – ask an adult for help.

SUN UNIT

 1 Sharpen both rod ends slightly. Mark 1.5 cm from one end of the rod, then push on the pulley until the mark just shows.

 2 Drill a hole, the same diameter as the rod, through the base. Smooth the base with sandpaper. Check that the rod turns easily in the hole.

1.5 cm

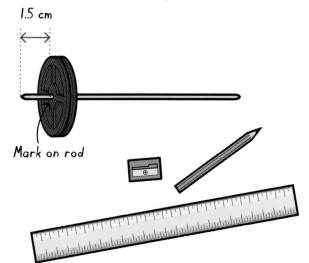

Mark on rod

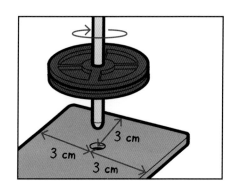

If the rod doesn't turn easily, run the drill through the hole again.

  3 Saw off 3 cm of wood to make a handle. Drill a hole, the same diameter as the rod, through the middle. Push the 1.5-cm rod end into the handle, as shown.

4 Hold the handle with one hand and rotate the base around it with the other. The base should turn easily, while the rod and pulley stay still.

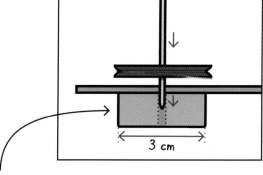

3 cm

Smooth all sides and edges of the handle with sandpaper.

If either the pulley or handle is loose on the rod, glue them on, but don't glue them to the base.

Rod and pulley should stay still.

Hold the handle still.

Push the base around.

5 Fit the rubber band over the pulley and lay it along the base. Mark a cross at the end. Remove the rubber band.

EARTH UNIT

 6 Mark a second cross 2 cm further along. At this mark, drill a 3.2-mm hole through the base to fit the first pop rivet.

Don't stretch the rubber band.

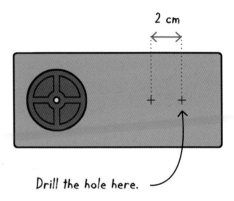

2 cm

Drill the hole here.

 7 Saw off 3 cm of wood, drill a 3.2-mm hole through the middle and smooth the edges. Push the thick end of the first pop rivet through the base into the wood.

 8 Draw round the bottle lid on the remaining wood. Saw roughly around the disc, then round it off using a file. Drill a 5-mm hole through the middle.

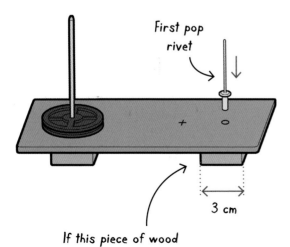

First pop rivet

3 cm

If this piece of wood is loose, glue it on.

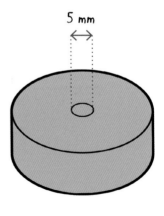

5 mm

Smooth any rough edges with sandpaper.

9 Push the motor pulley into the disc from one side and push the 5-mm tube in from the other side.

If anything is loose in its hole, glue it in, but don't get glue in the central hole or V-shaped groove of the pulley.

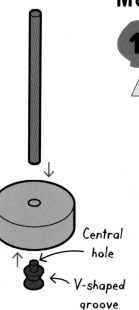

Central hole

← V-shaped groove

MOON UNIT

10 ⚠ Drill a 3.2-mm hole to one side of the tube, with the drill held at a slight angle. Push the thick end of the second pop rivet into the hole, as shown.

The slight angle of the hole is so the Moon doesn't touch Earth.

Second pop rivet

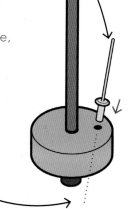

11 Glue the Moon onto the thick end of the third rivet. Join the two rivets together end to end with the thin tube, as shown.

If any rivets are loose, glue them in.

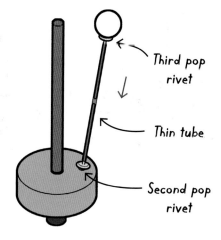

Third pop rivet

Thin tube

Second pop rivet

12 Slide the motor pulley onto the thin part of the first pop rivet in the base. Spin to check the unit rotates freely on the rivet.

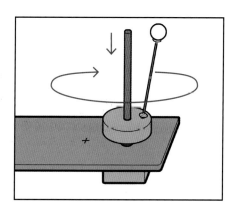

If the unit does not rotate freely, make sure there is no glue in the central hole.

FINISHING TOUCHES

 13 Push the Sun onto the rod. Sharpen one end of the skewer and push it into the Earth. Slide the other end into the 5-mm tube and glue in place.

 14 Lift the Earth unit off the first rivet. Place the rubber band around both pulleys and slide the unit back onto the rivet.

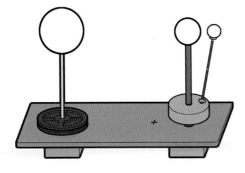

Adjust the Sun, Earth and Moon to roughly the same height.

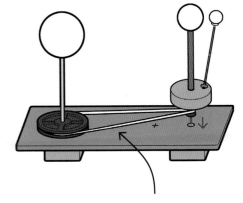

The rubber band should be slightly stretched.

 15 Hold the handle under the Sun with one hand and rotate the base around it with the other.

 16 Paint the Sun and Earth. You can also take the Earth/Moon unit off and paint the base black.

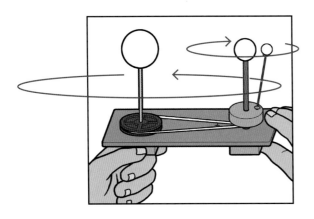

Earth should orbit the Sun, the Moon should orbit Earth, and Earth should spin about its axis.

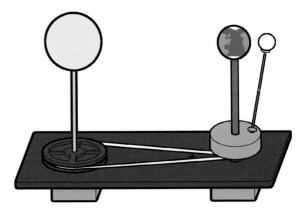

If the Sun, Earth or Moon come loose, glue them back on.

NOW YOU CAN...

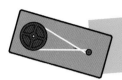

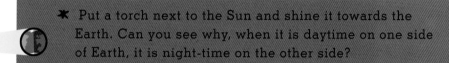

* Make the Moon orbit in the correct direction around Earth by fitting the rubber band in a figure-of-eight shape.

* Put a torch next to the Sun and shine it towards the Earth. Can you see why, when it is daytime on one side of Earth, it is night-time on the other side?

* Turn the motor pulley unit until the Moon is between the torch and Earth. Look at its shadow on Earth. When the Moon passes in between the Sun and Earth, making a shadow, this is known as a 'solar eclipse' (or eclipse of the Sun).

* Turn the motor pulley unit until Earth is between the torch and the Moon. The Moon will now be in shadow. This is known as a 'lunar eclipse' (or eclipse of the Moon).

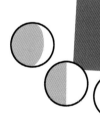

* Continue to turn the small pulley slowly and watch as the Moon comes out of the shadow of Earth. Can you see why the Moon appears to change shape as it orbits Earth?

HOW IT WORKS

When you hold the Sun still and rotate the base around it, you are making Earth orbit the Sun. In real life, this takes a year. At the same time the pulley arrangement is making the Moon orbit Earth, and Earth spin around on its own axis. Half of Earth is lit up by the Sun and the other half is in darkness. As Earth turns, the area where you live will go from light (daytime) to dark (night-time) and so on.

CONTROLLER SET-UP

YOU WILL NEED:

These parts are needed to connect up, power and communicate with the Crumble controller.

1 Crumble controller (from Redfern Electronics, see page 7)

2 bases e.g. hardboard, MDF, plywood, 3 mm thick x 6 cm x 9 cm

1 micro-USB cable

1 laptop computer

1 Crumble-friendly battery box 3 x AA (from Redfern Electronics, see page 7)

3 AA cells

2 crocodile leads

FROM YOUR TOOLBOX:

• Double-sided foam sticky tape • scissors

Here's how to set up the Crumble controller for the traffic lights, chair-o-plane and motorized buggy.

 1 Attach the Crumble to a base using a double layer of foam sticky tape along the centre on the side without components.

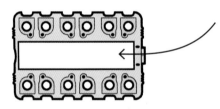

The double layer of tape will raise the controller enough for you to connect the crocodile clips to the terminals.

2 Push the small connector on your micro-USB cable into the socket at the end of the Crumble. Push the large connector into a USB socket on your laptop.

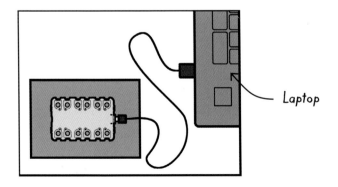

Laptop

3 Download and run the software from the Crumble controller website. Starting with the 'Basic' menu shown, drag and drop commands into the space on the right of your screen.

4 Write a program to switch on motor output 1 for a few seconds. Run it and check that the red LED next to motor output 1 comes on.

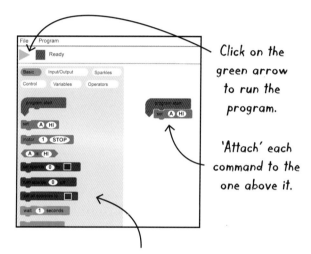

Click on the green arrow to run the program.

'Attach' each command to the one above it.

If you make a mistake you can drag and drop commands back into the left-hand section.

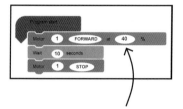

Click on the values in the white ovals to change them.

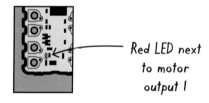

Red LED next to motor output 1

FOR THE CHAIR-O-PLANE AND MOTORIZED BUGGY

5 With the battery box switched off, fit the AA cells. Attach the battery box to the second base using two or more layers of foam sticky tape – this will raise the battery box enough for you to connect the crocodile clips to the terminals.

6 Use two crocodile loads to connect from the positive (+) and negative (-) terminals on the battery box to the positive and negative terminals next to the micro-USB connector, as shown.

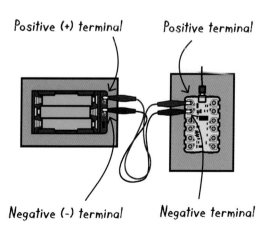

Positive (+) terminal   *Positive terminal*

Negative (-) terminal   *Negative terminal*

PROGRAM ME!

TrAFFIC LIGHTS

Make LED traffic lights and program them to come on in the right sequence.

YOU WILL NEED:

For the Crumble controller set-up see pages 98–99.

1 red LED
5–10-mm diameter

1 yellow LED
5–10-mm diameter

1 green LED
5–10-mm diameter

4 crocodile leads

For the fused bead traffic lights:

Fuse beads 5 mm

Large square pegboard for 5-mm fuse beads

For the cardboard traffic lights:

Corrugated cardboard
3–4 mm thick

FROM YOUR TOOLBOX:

• greaseproof paper • iron and ironing board • drill with drill bit the same diameter as your LEDs • low melt glue gun • pencil • ruler • large scissors • paint • paintbrush

⚠ **TAKE CARE** using the iron and drill – ask an adult for help.

Use the Crumble controller, base, micro-USB cable and laptop to set up your Crumble and write a simple program as described on pages 98–99. Now design your traffic lights using either fused beads or cardboard.

TO MAKE FUSED BEAD TRAFFIC LIGHTS...

 Lay out your design on the pegboard. Leave gaps to fit the LEDs. Include a base and support so it will stand up.

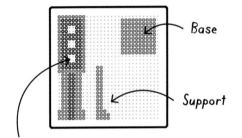

Base

Support

Leave out a single peg for a 5-mm LED or four pegs for a 10-mm LED.

 Cover your design with greaseproof paper and iron it at just below medium setting until the beads are well fused.

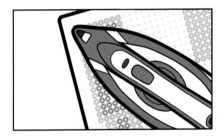

If the beads aren't well fused the design may split when you drill it.

 When cool, take the fused bead design off the pegboard, turn it over, cover it with greaseproof paper and iron again.

 Clamp your traffic light design, then drill out the holes to the same diameter as your LEDs. Glue the parts together.

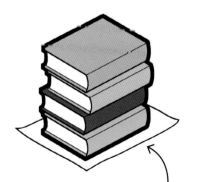

Place heavy books on top to stop the design distorting as it cools.

Glue the design to the base.

Glue the support to the back.

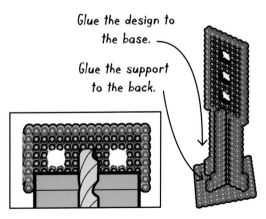

Try not to split your design while drilling.

TO MAKE CARDBOARD TRAFFIC LIGHTS...

 Draw and cut out a design from corrugated cardboard. Include a base and a support so your lights will stand up.

 To make the holes for the LEDs, push a pencil into the cardboard and rotate it.

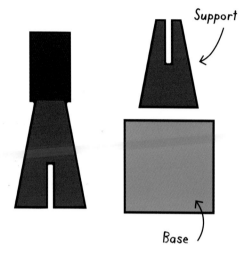

Support

Base

If using 5-mm LEDs, make sure they fit tightly in the holes.

 For large LEDs, such as 10 mm, push the shut blades of a pair of large scissors into each hole and rotate them to enlarge the holes until the LEDs just fit.

 Paint the parts and wait for them to dry, then slot them together and glue the stand to the base.

The large LEDs will need to fit tightly in the holes.

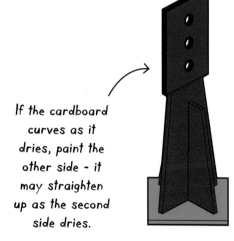

If the cardboard curves as it dries, paint the other side - it may straighten up as the second side dries.

COMPLETING THE TRAFFIC LIGHTS...

 10 Push in the LEDs. Gently bend the short legs of the red LED down and green LED up. Bend the short leg of the yellow LED in half, trapping the other two legs.

11 Clip one end of a crocodile lead onto all three linked short legs of the LEDs. Clip the other end to the negative (-) terminal on your Crumble, as shown.

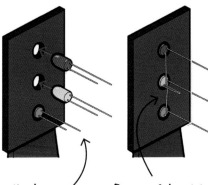
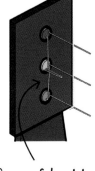

Make sure the long legs are all on the same side.

Be careful not to snap the legs when you bend them.

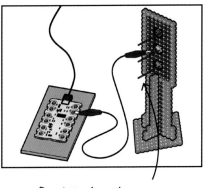

Bend the long legs away slightly so the crocodile clip doesn't touch them.

 12 Connect a crocodile lead from terminal A on the Crumble to the long leg of the red LED. Slide the leg into the plastic sleeve of the crocodile clip.

13 Connect a crocodile lead from terminal B to the long leg of the yellow LED. Connect the last crocodile lead from terminal C to the long leg of the green LED.

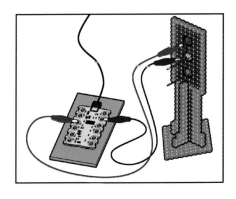

Make sure the metal clip doesn't touch the short leg of the LED.

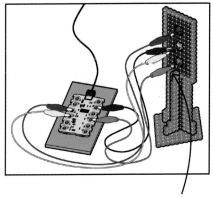

Slide the legs into the plastic sleeves of the crocodile clips.

PROGRAMMING THE TRAFFIC LIGHTS...

14 Start by writing a program to make just the red light continuously flash on and off for one second. Next, develop a program to switch the LEDs on and off, one after the other.

15 Now program a proper traffic light sequence. For example, in the UK the sequence is red (stop), red and yellow (get ready to go), green (go), yellow (get ready to stop), then back to the start again (red).

This is an example of a program to turn the red light on and off continuously.

Here is an example of a program that gives the UK light sequence.

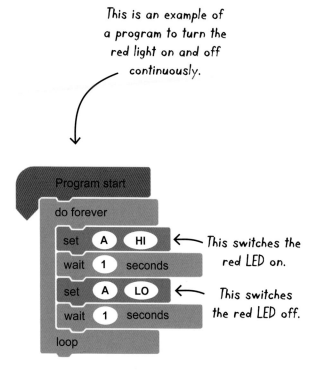

This switches the red LED on.

This switches the red LED off.

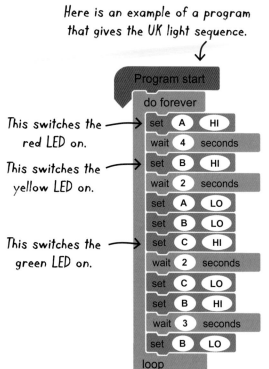

This switches the red LED on.

This switches the yellow LED on.

This switches the green LED on.

HOW IT WORKS

The Crumble controller is a circuit board that connects to the computer. The computer sends signals down the USB lead to the Crumble that tell it to set the output of each terminal either High or Low (indicated by HI or LO). When the output is High, the LED lights up.

NOW YOU CAN...

★ Adjust the timings of your traffic light sequence until you are happy with them.

★ Find out what the traffic light sequence is in another country (for example, France or the USA) and write a program for that.

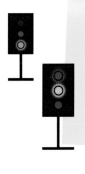

★ Get a friend to make a set of traffic lights, too. Use a crocodile lead to connect terminal D on the two Crumbles together. Write programs for the two sets of traffic lights, so that one remains on red until the other has completed its sequence and set output D to high (see program step below). The other traffic lights should wait for D to go high before starting the sequence. You don't want the cars to crash into one another!

★ Connect up an ultrasonic distance sensor and battery box (from Redfern Electronics, see page 7), then program your traffic lights so that they stay on red until a 'car' arrives. Connect terminal T (sensor) to terminal C (Crumble), and terminal E (sensor) to terminal D (Crumble).

You can use this command to wait for a signal from the distance sensor to say that a 'car' has arrived.

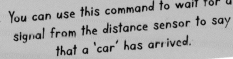

YOU WILL NEED:

For the Crumble controller set-up see pages 98–99.

1 motor

2 crocodile leads

1 plastic pot or bowl about 12–16-cm diameter

2 old CDs

1 plastic milk bottle lid

1 plastic drink bottle, lid about 4-cm diameter

1 pulley, 5-cm diameter

1 wooden rod to fit central hole in pulley

1 cork (preferably plastic)

Card, about 1.2 mm thick

1 rubber band 1.5 mm x 6 cm

1 motor mount

2 cable ties 25–30 cm long

Coloured A4 card

💀 💀
6 small toys (2–5 g)

FROM YOUR TOOLBOX:
• double-sided foam sticky tape • large scissors • low melt glue gun • poster tack • pencil • nail scissors • ruler • pencil sharpener • vice • junior hacksaw • drill with drill bit same diameter as wooden rod • sticky tape

PROGRAM ME!

CHAIR-O-PLANE

Construct an exciting fairground ride and control it using a simple program.

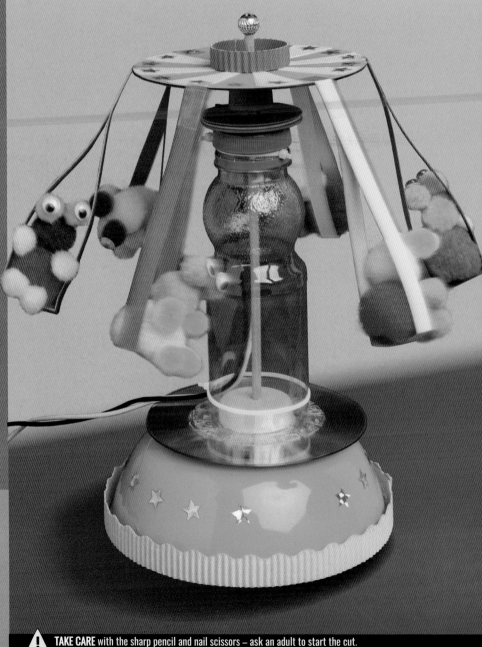

⚠ **TAKE CARE** with the sharp pencil and nail scissors – ask an adult to start the cut. Take care with the drill and saw – ask an adult for help.

1 Use the Crumble controller, two bases, micro-USB cable, laptop, battery box, three AA cells and two crocodile leads to set up and power your Crumble and write a simple program, as described on pages 98–99.

2 Connect the crocodile leads from motor output 1 on the Crumble to the motor terminals, as shown. Switch on, run the program and check the motor shaft rotates. Switch off and disconnect the motor.

3 ⚠ Make a hole in the milk bottle lid (see page 18, step 5). Widen it until the rod rotates easily in the hole. Turn the pot upside down and glue on a CD. Glue the lid on top, open end down.

Switch on here.

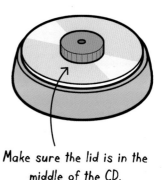

Make sure the lid is in the middle of the CD.

4 ⚠ Cut the bottom off the bottle. Cut flaps 1 cm long x 1.5 cm wide around the cut end and bend them out at right angles. Glue the bottle firmly to the CD.

5 ⚠ Unscrew the drinks bottle lid and draw around it on the thick card. Cut out the circle. Clamp the card disc in the vice and drill a hole in the middle.

Place the bottle centrally over the milk bottle lid.

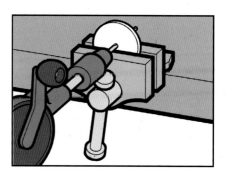

Make an indent first to help you drill in the right place.

Make a hole in the lid (see page 18, step 5). Widen the hole with the pencil until the rod can turn easily in the hole.

 Screw the lid back onto the bottle. Push the rod down through both lid holes until it touches the plastic pot. Mark the rod as shown.

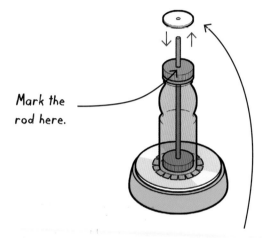

Mark the rod here.

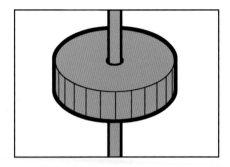

You can drill out the hole if necessary so that the rod turns easily.

Push the card disc down onto the rod to enlarge the hole, then remove it.

 Take the rod out and make a second mark 2 mm above the first one. Make a third mark 5 cm above this. Saw off at the third mark.

 Clamp the rod vertically and push the pulley down until it just touches the upper mark. Put the rod back into the bottle to check the pulley doesn't touch the lid, then remove the rod.

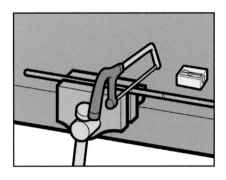

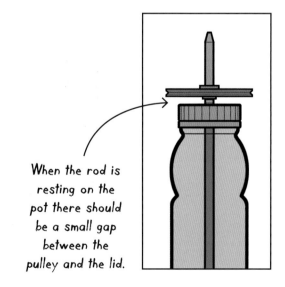

When the rod is resting on the pot there should be a small gap between the pulley and the lid.

Use a pencil sharpener to slightly sharpen both ends of the rod, but don't make them spiked.

10 Saw the cork in half. Drill a hole through one half and push it down the rod until it just touches the pulley. Glue the second CD to the cork.

11 Glue the top of the cork and CD inner circle, then push the card disc down firmly onto them. Fit the rubber band around the pulley and slide the rod back into the bottle.

Make sure the CD is central on the rod.

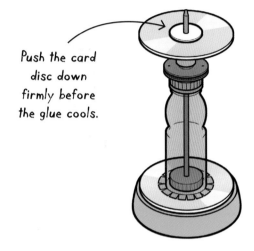

Push the card disc down firmly before the glue cools.

12 Clip the motor into the motor mount. Stick the mount to the side of the bottle lid, as shown. Line up the motor shaft with the V-shaped groove of the pulley.

13 Fix the motor and mount firmly in place with a cable tie. Cut off the loose end of the cable tie. Stretch the rubber band over the motor shaft.

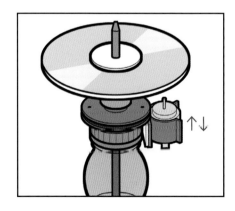

Adjust the height of the motor by pushing it up or down in its mount.

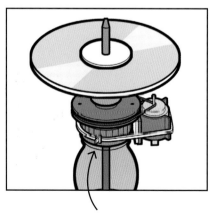

Trim the loose end of the cable tie short so that it won't catch on the chairs as they rotate.

14 Reconnect the crocodile leads to the motor terminals. Fit a cable tie around the bottom of the bottle. Switch on the battery box, run the program and check the CD rotates, then switch off.

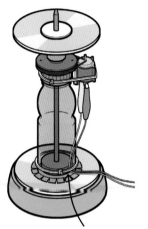

This cable tie is to keep the crocodile leads out of the way of the chairs.

15 Cut strips of card about 1 cm wide to make the chairs. Fold the strips around the toys and into long triangles, then tape the tops together, as shown.

Tape together.

Glue the toys to their chairs or make them seat belts from rubber bands or cable ties.

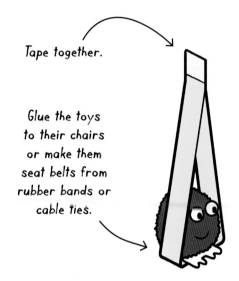

16 Tape each of the chairs to the CD. Try and put toys of equal weight opposite each other so that the ride is balanced. Switch on and watch the chair-o-plane swing your toys around.

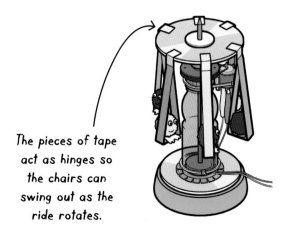

The pieces of tape act as hinges so the chairs can swing out as the ride rotates.

HOW IT WORKS

When the chair-o-plane is not moving, the chairs hang straight down due to gravity. When the chair-o-plane starts turning, the chairs swing outwards. As well as holding the toys up against the force of gravity, the chairs are now pulling the toys inward to make them travel round in a circle. As the chair-o-plane spins faster, more inward pull is needed, so the chairs fly out at a higher angle.

NOW YOU CAN...

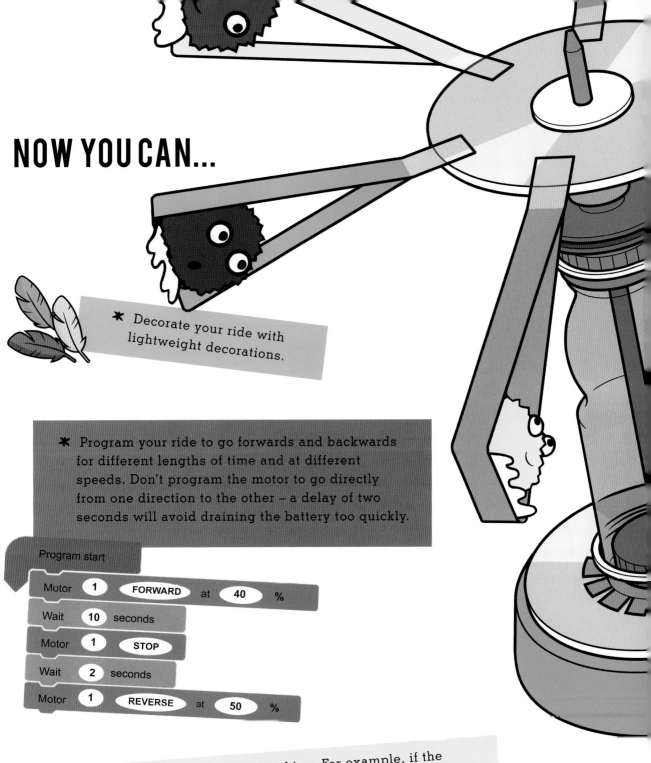

* Decorate your ride with lightweight decorations.

* Program your ride to go forwards and backwards for different lengths of time and at different speeds. Don't program the motor to go directly from one direction to the other – a delay of two seconds will avoid draining the battery too quickly.

Program start

| Motor | 1 | FORWARD | at | 40 | % |

| Wait | 10 | seconds |

| Motor | 1 | STOP |

| Wait | 2 | seconds |

| Motor | 1 | REVERSE | at | 50 | % |

* Fix your ride if it stops working. For example, if the rubber band keeps coming off the motor shaft, try sliding the motor up a little in its mount so that the rubber band runs near the bottom of the motor shaft.

PROGRAM ME!

MOTORIZED BUGGY

Create a driverless vehicle and program it to move, turn and park!

YOU WILL NEED:

For the Crumble controller set-up see pages 98–99.

4 crocodile leads

2 motors

2 motor mounts

Corrugated plastic or cardboard 3–4 mm thick x 30 cm x 30 cm

3 plastic drinking straws (loose fit on wooden rod)

1 wooden rod length 60 cm to fit holes in pulleys

2 pulleys 3–4-cm diameter

4 plastic milk bottle lids

2 rubber bands 1 mm x 1.5 mm x 6 cm

2 motor pulleys (see page 92)

10 small cable ties

2 medium cable ties about 20 cm long

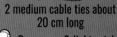
Passenger & lightweight decorations (optional)

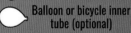
Balloon or bicycle inner tube (optional)

FROM YOUR TOOLBOX:

• marker pen • ruler • large scissors • junior hacksaw and vice • sharp pencil • poster tack • pencil sharpener • double-sided foam sticky tape

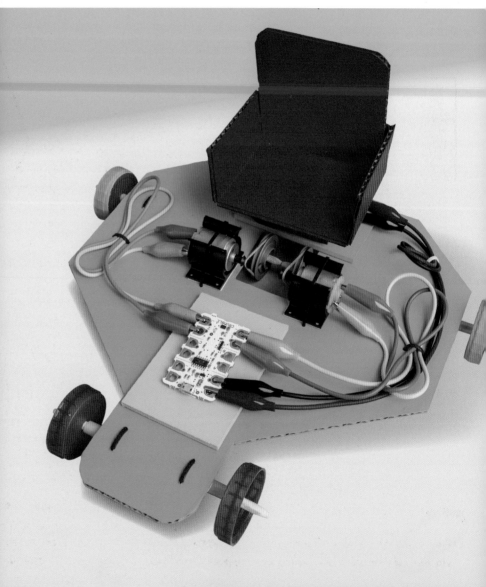

⚠ **TAKE CARE** with the sharp pencil.

1 Use the Crumble controller, two bases, micro-USB cable, laptop, battery box, three AA cells and two crocodile leads to set up and power your Crumble. Write a simple program, as described on pages 98–99.

2 Connect the positive (+) and negative (-) terminals of motor output 1 on the Crumble to the motor terminals. Connect motor output 2 to the second motor. Switch on.

3 Write a program to run both motors. An example is shown here. Run the program and check that both motor shafts rotate. Switch off and unplug the micro-USB cable.

Switch on the battery box here.

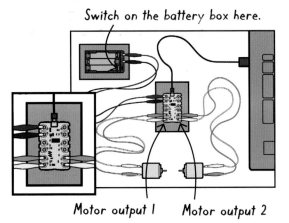

Motor output 1   Motor output 2

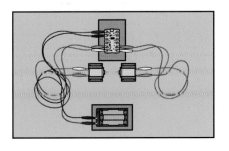

Run the motors on 50% power or less to start with, otherwise the Crumble may not have enough power to boot up.

4 Now understand how the buggy works. Each motor pulley drives a larger pulley on the driven axle using a rubber band. The straws allow the axles to rotate.

5 Clip the motors into the mounts and lay out the components on your corrugated sheet. Keep the weight towards the driven-wheels end to help them grip.

Non-driven axles and wheels rotate freely.

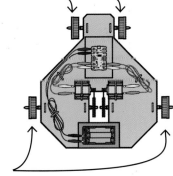

Driven axles and wheels are driven by the motor via the rubber band and pulley arrangement.

Keeping the weight near the driven wheels will allow the non-driven wheels to skid, enabling the buggy to turn.

Sketch a buggy base design on the corrugated sheet and cut it out. If mounting both pulleys in a central slot, make the slot at least 4 cm wide.

 Cut a length of straw to overlap the buggy base as shown. Cut a rod 5 cm longer than the straw. Make a hole in each wheel (see page 18, step 5).

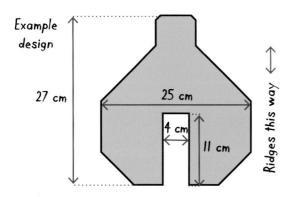

The corrugated ridges should run along the buggy to reduce bending.

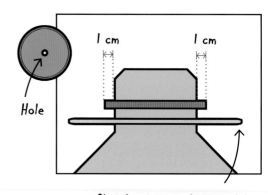

Slightly sharpen both ends of the rod.

8 Tape the straw to the underside of the base. Slide the rod through the straw and push the wheels on, open ends outwards, as shown. They should fit tightly on the rod.

9 Pierce holes on either side of the tape, as shown. Feed small cable ties through and fasten them gently around the straw to stop it moving. Make sure the axle still rotates freely.

Leave a small gap between the wheels and the straw.

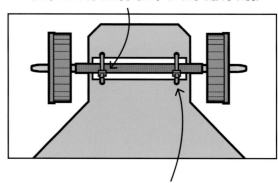

Hold the base and spin the wheels to check that the axle rotates freely.

Trim off the loose ends of the cable ties.

Don't pull the cable ties tight or they will crush the straw onto the axle and stop it rotating.

10 To fit a driven wheel, cut a piece of straw that overlaps the base as shown. Cut a rod 4 cm longer than the straw, push the pulley on 1 cm from the end and slide through the straw. Position on the base and mark.

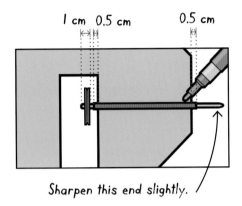

1 cm 0.5 cm   0.5 cm

Sharpen this end slightly.

11 Push on a wheel until there is a 1-mm gap between the end of the straw and the wheel. Attach the straw with foam tape, then secure it gently with cable ties.

Leave a small gap.

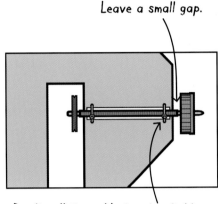

Don't pull the cable ties too tight.

12 Repeat steps 10 and 11 to fit the second driven wheel. Make sure you leave a gap between the two rods. Turn the base over.

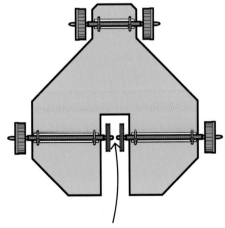

Check that there is a gap between the two rods.

13 Disconnect the motors and fit the motor pulleys. Place a rubber band over each pulley pair. Stretching the bands slightly, stick the motor mounts to the base and cable tie firmly.

If the rubber bands touch the end of the slot, cut a deeper slot.

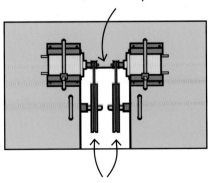

The V-shaped grooves of each pulley pair must be in line to stop the rubber band from coming off.

14 Stick the Crumble and battery box units to the buggy base and re-connect the motors. Switch on and check that both driven wheels rotate forwards. Switch off.

Tidy the wires neatly and cable-tie them to the base.

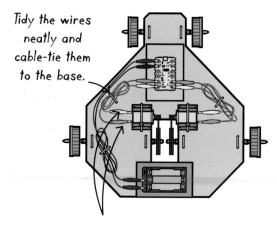

If your wheel goes backwards, swap these crocodile clips over to make it go forwards.

16 Click on the green arrow to download the program to the Crumble. Unplug the micro-USB lead, place your buggy on the floor and switch on to try out your program.

15 Place the buggy on a smooth floor, switch on and check that it moves forwards. Switch off again, re-connect the micro-USB lead and program the buggy to perform various moves, such as going forwards, backwards or spinning on its axis. An example is shown below.

Remember to start both the motors on 50 per cent power or less.

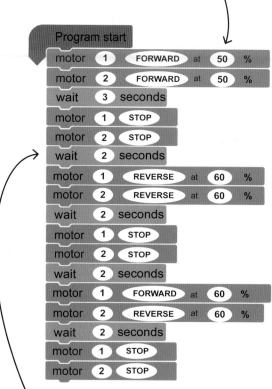

Program a delay when changing between forward and reverse to avoid draining the battery too quickly.

NOW YOU CAN...

* Decorate your motorized buggy and add a lightweight passenger.

* Program your buggy to do a three-point turn, parallel park or follow a course.

* Try racing a friend's buggy, or tie a string between the two and hold a tug of war. You could add tyres made of strips of balloon or bicycle inner tube to the driven wheels to help them grip.

HOW IT WORKS

The motors turn very fast, but have low torque (turning force), so you can't use them to drive the wheels directly. Instead, a small pulley on each motor shaft is used to drive a much larger pulley on the driven wheel axle, using a rubber band. This arrangement makes the wheels turn more slowly than the motor, but with a higher torque to propel (push) the buggy along. For example, if the motor pulley had a 3-mm diameter and the larger pulley had a 30-mm diameter, the larger pulley would rotate at about a tenth of the motor speed but would have about ten times the torque.

GLOSSARY

Axle A rod that passes through the centre of a wheel, enabling the wheel to rotate.

Cell/Battery An electrochemical cell converts chemical energy into electrical energy. A battery is two or more cells connected together. It is used to 'push' electricity round a circuit.

Centre of gravity If an object is hanging freely from a single point, it always comes to rest with the centre of gravity directly below that point. It is behaving as though all its weight is concentrated at its centre of gravity.

Compressed air Air is a gas. The particles in a gas are quite far apart compared with a solid or a liquid, so they can be squashed together (or compressed) into a smaller space.

Conductor An electrical conductor is a material that allows electricity to pass through it easily. Metal is a good conductor of electricity.

Elastic potential energy If you stretch a rubber band and then let go, the rubber band should return to its original shape. The type of energy stored in the stretched rubber band is called elastic potential energy.

Filter A colour filter is made from a material that allows only light of a certain colour to pass through it. For example, a red filter will only allow red light through – it will stop all the other colours.

Force A force can be a push or a pull. You can't see it, but you can often see its effect – a force can change the speed of an object, its direction of movement or its shape.

Friction A force between surfaces that are sliding, or trying to slide, across each other. Friction is often useful – for example, it stops bicycle tyres from slipping on the road.

Gear A rotating component with teeth that is used to drive another gear. If the two gears are different sizes, they will go round at different speeds.

Gravity A force that pulls things down and makes things fall to the ground. The more mass an object has, the more force will be pulling it down.

Insulator An electrical insulator is a material that does not allow electricity to pass through it. Plastic, wood and rubber are electrical insulators. Wires that carry electricity are often coated with plastic to make sure the electricity just flows along the wire.

Keel The part of a boat that sticks out from the bottom along its centre line. It helps the boat to go in the direction it is pointing.

Kinetic (movement) energy The energy an object has because it is moving. The faster an object moves, and the more mass it has, the more kinetic energy it will have.

Lift The force that pushes an aeroplane upwards to keep it in the air, opposing gravity, which is pulling it down towards the ground.

Load The force experienced by a structure. In the case of the lolly stick bridge, it is the weight it has to support.

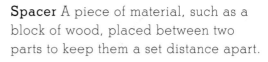

Negative electrical charge All objects are built of many tiny positively and negatively charged particles, normally equal in number. If the numbers become unbalanced, we say that the object has a positive or negative charge. Particles that are negatively charged will attract positively charged particles. If they are connected together by a conductor, the electrical charge will be able to flow through it.

Offset An offset is the distance by which something is out of line. In the vibrating brush monster, the offset on the rotating disc is the distance of the mounting hole from the centre of the disc.

Orbit To travel in a path around another object. For example, Earth orbits the Sun.

Positive electrical charge Positively charged particles are attracted to negatively charged particles. (Please see Negative electrical charge, above.)

Pressure Pressure is a pushing force spread over an area. Squeezing a sealed plastic bottle puts its contents under pressure. If it is full of air, the air can be squashed easily into a smaller space, whereas water cannot.

Reflection When light hits a smooth, shiny surface, such as a mirror, it bounces off. This is known as reflection.

Short circuit A circuit that allows electricity to flow round a path with very little resistance, so the battery will drain rapidly and get hot.

Spacer A piece of material, such as a block of wood, placed between two parts to keep them a set distance apart.

Streamlined A streamlined object has a shape designed to reduce resistance to movement through water or air, so that the object can pass through more easily and quickly.

Template A shaped piece of material used as a pattern for drawing or cutting around.

Torque A turning or twisting force acting on an object.

INDEX
